Longman

Popcorn

5

Teacher's Book

Brian Abbs • Anne Worrall • Ann Ward

Course summary

Unit	Topic	Language	
1 The competition	A photo competition	*Describing daily routines:*	Domino gets up at ...
			What time do you ...?
		Adverbs of frequency:	sometimes, usually, always
		Talking about the past:	What did Kate do last month?
			She read about the competition.
		Time expressions:	last month, three weeks ago, four days later, last week, this morning
2 Say cheese!	Cameras and photography	*Explaining how things work:*	How does ... work?
			When you (press a button), the ...
		Explaining problems:	Why is this person too small?
			Because he wasn't close enough to the camera.
		Talking about the past:	When did they build the camera obscura?
			Did you take this photograph?
3 Action!	At a movie studio The life of a stunt artist	*Talking about hobbies and skills:*	What does Donna do?
			She does skydiving.
		Expressing desires:	I'd like to ...
		Making suggestions:	Why don't you ...?
		Talking about needs and abilities:	They need ...
			Can ...?
Language review 1		*Simple Present:*	Do you play the tuba?
			Yes, I play every day.
		Simple past:	I played in a concert last week.
4 My favorite movies	Movie making and sound effects	*Talking about likes and dislikes:*	I like adventure stories.
			My favorite movies are ...
		Identifying people:	Who is this?
			It's one of the actors.
		Talking about ambitions:	What do you want to be?
		Identifying sounds:	What does this sound like?
			It sounds like a rainstorm.
		Asking for explanations:	How did you?
5 On location	Making a movie on location	*Talking about plans:*	Marina's going to escape from the ship.
			What am I going to do?
		Expressing a preference:	I'd rather ...
6 A famous pirate	Pirates in history	*Describing past events:*	Blackbeard attacked many treasure ships.
			Where did ...?
		Adverbs of frequency:	They often ...; They never ...
Language review 2		*Asking questions about the past:*	Who did you go with?
			Where did you go?
			What did you see?
			When did you go?
			How many .../How much ...?
7 Sam's disappeared!	Adventures under the ocean	*Describing recent events:*	What's happened?
			Sam's disappeared.
			What have they done?
8 Under the ocean	The ocean and marine life	*Describing a place:*	There are high mountains under the ocean.
		Adverbs of manner:	Jellyfish float gently near the surface of the ocean.
		Making comparisons:	The blue whale is the largest creature on earth.
		Narrating a story in the past:	It was a dark night. The wind blew strongly.

Unit	Topic	Language	
9 **Sam's discovery**	Finding treasure under the ocean	*Past ability:*	Could Sam escape? No he couldn't.
		To and enough:	It's too small. It isn't big enough.
Language review 3		*Comparatives and superlatives:*	The sperm whale is bigger than the humpback whale. The blue whale is the biggest. Who's the tallest person in the class?
10 **Mysteries of the ocean**	Unsolved mysteries	*Expressing facts:*	Over fifth ships have disappeared.
		Expressing opinions:	Perhaps there is a strong force ...
		Talking about experiences:	Have you ever been on a ship?
11 **Jake Jones's diary**	A diary of a journey	*Describing when and where things happened:*	When did she have the history test? Four days ago. Where were you two days ago?
		Likes and dislikes:	He likes eating but he hates cooking.
12 **What kind of music do you like?**	Pop music and musical instruments	*Likes and dislikes:*	I like reggae, but I don't like pop music.
		Abilities:	I can play the flute.
		Desires and ambitions:	I'd like to play the trumpet. What would you like to be? I'd like to be a video director.
		Interests:	What are you interested in? I'm interested in football.
		Sequencing events:	First ..., then ..., next ..., after that ..., finally ...
Language review 4		*Present perfect:*	I've painted the walls yellow. Have you finished?
13 **Can we speak to Rick Morell, please?**	A chase across the desert	*Requests:*	Can we have our ball back, please?
		Describing location:	Where's the duck? It's in the middle of the pond.
		Narrating events in the past:	First we saw ...
14 **A trip around the world**	Traveling and transportation	*Talking about the past:*	We visited the pyramids in Egypt.
		Making plans for a trip:	Let's go to ... Do you want to go to ...? OK. And then we'll go to ...
		Making predictions:	People will travel by ...
		Asking for explanations:	I'm going to take my walkman. Why? Because ...
15 **Buried treasure**	Digging for treasure	*First conditional:*	If we follow Jake's map we'll find the treasure. What'll happen if ...
		Talking about measurements:	How deep was the first thing they found? How long did it take ...?
Language review 5		*First conditional:*	If he opens the window, the bird will escape. What'll happen if it rains?
16 **The end of the story**	Discovering the treasure. Time capsules	*Talking about plans:*	I'm going to ... Would you like to ...? I'd like to ...
Language review 6		*Past, present and future:*	My sister taught me to play the guitar. Do you practice every day? I'm going to make a record.

Introduction

1 Aims of the course

Popcorn is the elementary course which helps you and your pupils get the most out of English.

Popcorn uses children's creative energy as a classroom resource. The aim is to encourage children to develop language and educational skills and to enjoy the learning process. Children's natural interests are engaged and maintained through lively stories, interesting topic work and a variety of activities, including projects, games and songs.

The topics have been chosen for their interest and appropriateness to children of this age. Language learning is combined with general educational skills. **Popcorn** incorporates work from other areas of the school curriculum and offers a range of opportunities to learn about other cultures and ways of life.

Popcorn has a realistic syllabus with constant recycling so that pupils become familiar and confident with what they have learned. The course gives plenty of practice in the four skills of speaking, listening, reading and writing.

2 Teaching English to children – general guidelines

Creative use of language

Allow your pupils' natural imaginative instinct to make them active learners. Children should be encouraged to use English creatively, to experiment with the language they are learning and to apply it to various situations. Games, puzzles, pairwork and groupwork encourage children to work together and to solve problems for themselves.

Mistakes

In the course of experimenting with the language, children will make mistakes. This is a natural and useful part of the learning process. Mistakes should not therefore be corrected in ways that discourage pupils from trying out new ways of using language. Too much emphasis on accuracy can be inhibiting. During a game, for example, it is not appropriate or possible to correct all mistakes as they occur. It is better to make a note of persistent mistakes and work on them later.

In many of the oral exercises, the teacher's task is to help pupils to express what they need to say rather than correct mistakes. On the other hand, some exercises, such as the written exercises in the Activity Book or the model dialogs, are designed to improve accuracy. These can be corrected and mistakes discussed in more detail.

Settling down and brightening up

You will find that different types of activities have different effects on pupils.

In general, activities involving writing, drawing, reading and listening have a settling effect. Many of the Activity Book exercises fall into this category. Games, songs and some oral activities animate pupils and brighten them up after a quiet session.

It is useful to have some settling down and brightening up activities on hand so that you can vary the mood of your class.

It may be advisable to change the order of the activities in the lesson notes sometimes to fit in with your pupils' mood, e.g. if they arrive in an excitable mood and you want to help them settle down.

Use of L1

Your aim should be to use as much English as possible in the class. Introduce English classroom language from the beginning. Help pupils to correct themselves when they say something in L1 that they should be able to say in English, e.g. *Thank you.* Try to get pupils used to the idea that certain times in the lesson are "English only" times, for example, when doing pairwork.

Use L1 to ask questions about the background of stories and new situations to make your pupils more interested in them. Avoid explaining grammar rules: these are too difficult for young pupils and at this stage are unnecessary.

3 Organization of the course and teaching methods

The course consists of 16 units and 6 Language review units of 4 lessons each, providing material for up to 88 teaching hours, although this can be adapted to your needs. The course contains:
- Pupils' Book
- Activity Book
- A set of two class cassettes
- Teacher's Book

Pupils' Book

In **Popcorn 5**, pupils follow an exciting storyline in which two American schoolchildren have an adventure searching for buried treasure. Each alternate unit is a special topic unit, where pupils can explore cross-curricular themes and topics of interest such as movies, pirates and music in more detail.

New language is presented in context at the beginning of each unit – in the story dialogs, or in the topic presentation texts.

There is a variety of practice activities, including games, a listening exercise, pairwork, rhymes and songs. The Pupils' Book exercises focus on speaking, listening and reading.

Listening exercises are indicated by the symbol 🎦, pairwork by the symbol 😊, and personalization exercises by the symbol your turn! .

A special fun feature is the animated "flick" picture of a dolphin at the top right-hand corner of each page. Let pupils discover for themselves that if they flick the book, he moves.

Activity Book

Pupils consolidate what they have learned with exercises and puzzles involving writing, listening, reading, speaking and drawing and coloring.

Alternate units of the Activity Book have a project or craft activity lesson. Projects are indicated by the symbol ✏️ and crafts by the symbol ✂️. The Teacher's Book gives ideas on how to use these lessons for a variety of language activities.

The cassettes

The cassettes contain a recording of the story in the Pupils' Book, complete with sound effects, the listening exercises for the Pupils' Book and Activity Book, the model dialogs for pupils to use in the pairwork activities and the songs and rhymes.

Teacher's Book

The Teacher's Book provides step-by-step lesson notes. Suggestions are also given for extension and project work which will help your pupils expand their language work to reflect broader spheres and other curriculum subjects. Not all the ideas have to be taken up. You might like to select projects which fit in with the work pupils are doing in other parts of the curriculum.

Three photocopiable tests are also provided at the back of the Teacher's Book. These can be used at the end of each semester.

4 Guidelines on specific activities

Pupils may take some time to get used to new kinds of activities. Make sure that they understand what is expected of them and give a little time to allow them to feel confident. The following guidelines suggest procedures for certain common activities.

Pairwork

Pairwork allows pupils to make maximum use of classroom time. It increases the time they spend speaking and ensures that they contribute to the class. The following steps will help you to set it up:

- Make sure that pupils are familiar with all the language that they need for the activity.

- Select pairs.

- Give the instructions and make sure pupils have understood, using gestures.

- Demonstrate the activity using a couple of pairs of pupils.

- Start the activity. Monitor (go round the class listening, helping and encouraging where necessary. You could also make a mental note of difficulties for further review work).

It can be more settling for pupils to work with a regular partner but it can vary the activity if you get pupils to work with new partners. Finding a new partner can be a useful language exercise in itself! You can arrange it as a game by giving each pupil half of a matching pair and asking them to find their partner, e.g. half a picture, or a question and an answer, or a picture and a word.

Groupwork

When they work in groups, pupils should be able to see each other and interact, so they should be grouped around a table or with their desks pushed together. Similar steps to those for pairwork should be followed for setting up the activity.

Teaching vocabulary

Use the pictures in the book and objects in the class to teach new vocabulary.

- Point to the picture/object and try to elicit the new word from the pupils first.

- Say the word and ask pupils to repeat.

- Write the new word on the board.

- Check they have understood by asking them to point to the correct picture/object.

Direct translation can be useful with more abstract vocabulary but should be avoided if possible.

Help your pupils to remember new words by storing them in an ordered way. Pupils can be encouraged to make a picture dictionary or to keep a vocabulary book.

The story

Popcorn 5 has an exciting storyline which can be exploited as follows:

- Engage children's interest by looking at the pictures and asking them about them in English or L1.

- Teach key words if they are essential to general understanding. Not all new language should be highlighted at this point though. Let the pupils hear and see it in the context of the story first.

- Play the cassette while pupils listen and follow in their books.

- Ask a few simple questions (in English or L1) to check comprehension.

- Play the cassette again for pupils to listen and repeat. Pupils will enjoy this more if they are really encouraged to "act" what they are repeating – copying the intonation and perhaps repeating the sound effects!

- Pupils can read the dialog in pairs or groups. They could also act it out in front of the class, with props if possible.

Topic units

The topic units allow pupils to explore real-life topics that are related to the story. The material can be used as follows:

- Ask pupils in English or L1 what they already know about the topic. For example, if the topic is music, you can ask what sort of music do you like, who's your favorite pop star, etc.

- Ask pupils to look at the pictures in the Pupils' Book and tell you in English or L1 what is happening.

- Play the presentation texts on cassette while pupils listen and follow in their books.

- Ask a few simple questions in English to check comprehension.

- Select one or two items of information for extension work. For example, in the topic unit about music, you could focus their attention on musical instruments and ask them what their favorite instrument is and why. Or you could ask them to make a list of the musical instruments that people in the class play.

Model dialogs

Many of the Pupils' Book exercises have model dialogs on the cassette.

- Talk about the pictures in English or L1. Teach any new words.

- Play the cassette and ask pupils to repeat.

- Put the pupils into pairs.

- Ask a couple of pairs to demonstrate the dialog.

- Pairs practice together while you monitor.

Pupils can make up extra dialogs of their own and extra dialogs can be made using the material in the Activity Book.

Songs

Besides being enjoyable for the pupils, songs are invaluable for practicing intonation and pronunciation. They can be exploited in a number of ways. Here is a standard procedure.

- Talk about the pictures in English or L1. Pupils can try to guess what the song is about. Teach any key words.

- Play the song on cassette. Pupils listen. They can start humming the tune as it becomes familiar.

- Play the song again, line by line, pausing for pupils to repeat.

- Play the song again and let pupils sing along.

- In addition, pupils can be divided into groups to sing alternate verses, asked to mime the actions of the song as they sing, even to write their own verses! Pupils will often want to hear their favorite songs again and again.

Note: Sometimes the songs contain structures and vocabulary that are more advanced than the language pupils have been learning. This is a useful way of exposing them to more language receptively. Explain the meaning of the song and of individual words, but there is no need to teach this language in a formal way.

Games

Games channel children's natural instinct for fun into successful language learning!

As with pairwork and groupwork make sure that pupils understand the activity and demonstrate with groups of pupils first. Play the games again and again, to review language and to vary the pace of lessons. Pupils will probably enjoy some of the games more the second time they play – as they become more confident and know the rules.

Project work

Projects encourage pupils to take an active role in exploring topics further and to relate what they are learning in English to other parts of the curriculum.

The topic material in the Pupils' Book gives ideas of different ways that pupils can present their projects. Further project ideas are suggested in the Activity Book and Teacher's Book.

Pupils can do projects in groups, collecting material for a poster or a file on the subject.

Project posters should be displayed in the class. If possible, an area of the classroom wall should be set aside for pupils' drawings and writing in English, which can be used as a teaching aid.

Craft activities

Children will enjoy these craft activities where they learn English as they make something.

The materials needed for these activities are listed in the Activity Book and in the Teacher's Book. Work out how many you need before the lesson.

If you have time, it would also be helpful to have prepared a sample of the object they are going to make (projector, poster etc.) before the class. This will help you to make sure that the materials you have are suitable (the right weight of cardboard, the right type of glue, etc.) and to foresee any difficulties your pupils may experience.

- Make sure pupils understand what they have to do by demonstrating – either with the object you have made before the class, or by mime. Use English throughout – your demonstration should make the meaning clear.
- Divide pupils into groups. Make sure that each group have the necessary materials.
- Go around the class helping and encouraging.

Pronunciation

Pronunciation and intonation is practiced through songs and rhymes and by listening and repeating material on the cassette.

Spelling

The written activities and puzzles in the Activity Book will help you to check pupils' spelling. You can make it more fun by giving pupils anagrams to solve, by playing hangman or by giving out alphabet cards and asking pupils to make words.

Cultural awareness

The pictures and photos in **Popcorn** can be used to teach children about life in other countries.

- Ask pupils to look at the picture/photo and tell you (L1) what things they can see that are different from things in their own country.
- Ask pupils to tell you what else they know about the country/people shown.
- Pupils can imagine what it's like to spend a day as the people in the pictures.
- Pupils can draw pictures of similar scenes in their own countries. You can encourage pupils to make a "cultural file" with their drawings (labeled) and pictures from magazines.

5 Materials needed

We have kept extra materials needed to a minimum.

Much of the pupils' writing will be in the Activity Book. In addition to this, pupils are asked to draw and write about aspects of their own lives. For this they will need colored pencils and sheets of paper. The drawings should be kept for question and answer sessions and for display in the class. They can also be kept by pupils in a loose-leaf folder, which will be more useful than an exercise book.

Apart from the materials needed for the Craft Activities (see above) the following teaching aids would be useful:

Flashcards

These are cards you prepare with writing or pictures on. They can be used to introduce and review new language. They should be drawn/written on stiff cardboard and be big enough for pupils to see/read when you hold them up.

Magazine pictures

Pictures from magazines can also be mounted on cardboard to be used as a visual aid. It is often difficult to find the right pictures just before you need them, so cut out and keep pictures you think will be useful and save them for use later in the course. Pictures we have found useful include pictures of families doing different things in the home, animals, food, people of different ages, transportation and clothes.

Magazine pictures can also act as extra cultural background material, as can any English "realia" material – tourist brochures, English comics, etc.

Objects

Real objects (a map or a globe, clothes, toy cars, etc.) often help to focus pupils' attention and make vocabulary more meaningful to pupils.

6 Charting progress

As the course progresses, you (and parents!) will want to see how your pupils are getting on. Their performance in class will give you a good idea but progress can be monitored in a number of ways. Assessment should be approached sensitively, so that pupils are not discouraged by bad results.

Assessment activities

At the end of the lesson notes for each unit in the Teacher's Book there is a suggestion for an activity which will help you to assess informally if pupils have grasped the main language points of the unit. These activities should be fitted into a normal lesson when time permits.

An assessment chart

You can make a chart to record progress. This can be filled in with numbers or with symbols:

name	Assessment 1	Assessment 2	Assessment 3
Ana	1	2	1
Claudia	2	3	2
Niklas	2	1	1

1 = very good, 2 = good, 3 = needs attention

Informal assessment

In class, you can assess pupils informally by asking extra questions to individual pupils as you go around the class while they are doing pairwork to make sure that all pupils know what is going on.

It is also worthwhile to observe the way pupils perform in pairwork or groupwork, to identify those who seem to be struggling.

Tests

There are three tests at the back of the Teacher's Book. These can be photocopied. They include a listening test (which the teacher reads), and reading and writing exercises. The teacher's script for the listening tests and the key to the exercises are on page 92 of the Teacher's Book.

Pupils should do these tests individually. Make sure that pupils do not feel intimidated by these tests; their main purpose is to show you which areas need further work.

Putting things right

If the assessment shows that most of the class have performed badly, repeat relevant exercises in the Pupils' Book, ask additional oral questions and practice writing sentences using the language point. Then do the assessment activity again.

If some pupils are consistently performing badly, give them some extra attention in class, sitting in and helping them with their pairwork. It sometimes helps to change their partners for pairwork.

7 Classroom language

The following classroom language will help to conduct most of your class in English.

Greetings
Hello/Hi.
Good morning.
Good morning, Miss Fisher.

Basic instructions
Watch.
Watch carefully.

Listen.
Listen carefully.

Look.
Look at this.
Look at page 10.
Look at picture 2.
Listen and look.

Point.
Point to Ben.
Point to the dog.
Point to the right picture.

Touch.
Touch your desk.
Touch something blue.
Listen and touch the right thing.

Read.
Read this word.
Read the story.
Read this page.
Read the part of Ben.
Read the words and match the pictures.

Draw.
Draw a picture.
Draw a picture of Elvis.
Draw a picture and color it.

Show me.
Show me something blue.
Show me your pictures.
Hold up your pictures.

Write.
Write the words.

Tell the class.
Tell me about your family.
Tell us about Ben.
Tell your friend about your picture.
Who can tell me the answer? Hands up!

Organizing the class
Sit down, please.
Stand up, please.
Come here.
Work in pairs.
Work in groups.
In pairs, please.
In groups, please, everyone.
Close the door, please.
Can you close the door, please?
Open the window, please, Sally.
Take out your books.
Where's your book, Susannah?
Do you have a pencil, Jenny?
Do you all have a pencil?

Changing activities
Let's play a game.
Do you want to play a game now?
Start now!
Stop now!
Let's sing a song.
Who can sing this song?
Let's act this story.
You can be Jill and you can be Eddy.

Taking turns
Whose turn is it?
It's my turn.
It's your turn.
It's Cathy's turn.

Can I read now?
All right, Alex.

Will you read, please, Fiona?
You can read now, Jenny.
Who wants to read now?

Can I go to the bathroom, please?
OK. Be quick.

Quickly and quietly
Quickly, everyone.
Come on, James.
Sh! Quiet!
Keep quiet, please.
Quietly, please.
Don't do that, Catherine!

Questions about language
What's this in English?
It's "cat".

How do you spell it?
C–A–T.

Who can spell "banana" in English?
Me!

How do you say "pizza" in English?
You say "pizza"!

Praise
Good!
That's good!
Very good!
What a nice picture!
That's very good!
Almost right, Ann, try again.

Activity lessons

Cut.
Cut out the squares.

Glue.
Glue the squares together.

Make.
Make a robot.

Some scissors, some glue, some paper, some string.
I need a piece of paper.
I need some glue.

Finishing up
Time to stop now.
Collect the books, Jack.
Put your books away.
Who can be ready first?

At the end of the lesson
See you tomorrow.
See you on Monday.
Goodbye, everyone.
Bye bye.

Unit 1   The competition

Background information

In Popcorn 4 pupils followed the exciting adventures of two American schoolchildren, Kate and Sam Roberts, who went to the rain forest in Indonesia to find a rare plant. In Popcorn 5 Sam and Kate are back at school, about to start a new adventure. In Unit 1, they have just seen a poster on the school bulletin board advertising an exciting photography competition.

Lesson 1

Language	New words and expressions
Present simple *Adverbs of frequency*	bulletin board, photography, photo essay, competition, title, movie studio, entry, enter, star, early, shed, wildlife, sometimes, usually, something nice to eat, something special
Materials needed model clock	

Beginning the lesson

- Ask pupils to find out how much they know about their friends. Tell them to ask each other questions: *How old is (Maria)? Does she like parties? What's her favorite color?* etc.

- If pupils have used **Popcorn 4**, ask them to look at the pictures of the children on the cover and title page of the Pupils' Book and tell you who they are, and what they can remember (in L1) about their adventures in Indonesia.

- If pupils have not used **Popcorn 4**, ask them to look at the pictures of the children and guess what their names are, how old they are, etc. (Kate is thirteen and Sam is twelve. Kate has a cat called Domino, and Sam has a dog called Beano.) Pupils will find out about the two adult characters later in the story.

The competition

Kate and Sam are looking at the school bulletin board.

- Open Pupils' Books at page 2 and discuss the story in L1. Ask pupils to tell you where the people in the pictures are and what they are doing. Teach the new word *competition*.

 Listen to the cassette. Pupils follow the story in the Pupils' Book.

- Teach the rest of the new vocabulary as you ask questions about the story: *What are Kate and Sam looking at? What kind of competition is it? Who wants to enter the competition?* etc.

 Play the cassette again, pausing for pupils to repeat.

- Pupils read the story again in pairs.

Domino's day

Read and match

- Teach the new vocabulary: *something nice to eat, something special, shed, wildlife, sometimes* and *usually.*

- Ask pupils to read about Domino's day and match the actions with the pictures.

- Ask questions about Domino's day: *Does Domino get up early? Who does he meet? What time does he have his breakfast? Where does he have his breakfast?* etc.

What does Domino do?

Listen and answer the questions.

 Play the cassette, pausing for pupils to listen and answer the questions.

Tapescript and key

Sam: What does Domino do early in the morning?
(He gets up.)
What does he do at eight o'clock?
(He has his breakfast.)
What does he do in the middle of the morning?
(He visits his friend, Mrs. Tucker.)
And what does he do in his secret place on top of the shed?
(He sleeps.)
What does he sometimes do in the afternoon?
(He rides with Sam on his bike. Sometimes he plays the piano.)
What does he have at dinner time?
(He usually has cat food, but sometimes he has something special.)
And what does he sometimes do in the evenings?
(He watches television.)

- Check the answers by asking the questions to the whole class.

 Play the cassette again, pausing for pupils to listen and repeat.

- Ask pupils to ask each other questions about Domino's day:
  A: What time does he have his breakfast?
  B: Eight o'clock.
  A: When does he visit Mrs.Tucker? etc.

Ending the lesson

- Ask pupils to practice telling the time by asking and answering questions with the model clock. *What time is it? (It's ten after eight.)* etc.

Lesson 2

Language	New words and expressions
Present simple	catch (the bus), practice,
Time expressions	choir, pony, trumpet, clean
Materials needed	
model clock	

Beginning the lesson

- Practice telling the time with the model clock.

 What do they do?

Read and match.

- Discuss life in the country and life in the city in L1: *Which is better? What kind of things can you do in the country that you can't do in the city? Do people in the country spend more time out of doors? Do they get up earlier?*

- Ask pupils to read what the two people do and to say which are Alison's activities and which are Peter's.

- Ask questions: *Who goes to school by bike? (Peter.) How does Alison go to school? (She catches the school bus.) Who goes swimming? (Peter.)* etc.

 Play the cassette. Pupils listen and match the times with the activities.

Tapescript and key

Interviewer: Hello, what's your name?
Alison: Alison.
Interviewer: Tell us about your day, Alison. What do you do every day?
Alison: Well, I get up at seven-thirty and have my breakfast. Then I feed my pony at about eight-thirty. He's always very hungry.

Interviewer: What time do you go to school?
Alison: I catch the school bus at twenty to nine and I arrive at school at nine o'clock. I have lessons in the morning and I have lunch at quarter to one.
Interviewer: What do you do in the afternoon?
Alison: I practice with the school choir at two o'clock and then I have more lessons. Then I go home and ride my pony. I usually ride my pony at about a quarter to four.
Interviewer: What time do you have dinner?
Alison: At about seven o'clock. Then I practice my trumpet. I practice my trumpet every day. It's very difficult.
Interviewer: And what time do you go to bed?
Alison: At about nine-thirty.
Interviewer: And now Peter. What time do you get up, Peter?
Peter: I also get up at about seven-thirty.
Interviewer: And what do you do after that?
Peter: I clean my room!
Interviewer: Really?
Peter: Yes. Then I go to school at ten to nine. I go to school by bike.
Interviewer: Do you have lunch at school?
Peter: Yes, I have lunch at a quarter to one. After lunch I practice football with the school team, then lessons start again at two o'clock.
Interviewer: Do you like sports?
Peter: Yes, I do. I go swimming every day after school, too. I usually go swimming at about four o'clock.
Interviewer: What do you do in the evenings?
Peter: I have dinner at about six-thirty. Then at seven-thirty I usually make model airplanes. I'm making a jumbo jet at the moment. Then at nine o'clock I go to bed.

- Ask questions with the whole class: *What time does Alison get up? Does Peter get up early?* etc.

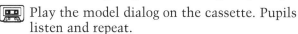 Play the model dialog on the cassette. Pupils listen and repeat.

- Pupils talk about Alison and Peter in pairs.

 Write about your day.

- Look at the exercise with the whole class. Do a sample day on the board with the whole class.

- Pupils fill in details about their own lives. Help them with vocabulary.

- Pupils talk to their partners about their days.

- Pupils can draw pictures of their weekend activities and talk about them with their partners or groups: (*This is my family on Sunday morning. We usually ...*) etc.

Ending the lesson

- Ask questions with the whole class: *What do you usually have for breakfast on the weekend? Do you get up early on Sundays? What time do you get up on schooldays?* etc.

Lesson 3

> **Language**
> What time do you ...?
> *Present simple*
> *Time expressions*
> *Past simple*
> When did you last...?
>
> **New words and expressions**
> last + week, month, year etc.
>
> **Materials needed**
> a model clock

Beginning the lesson

- Review times with the model clock. Ask a pupil to turn the clock hands and ask: *What do you do at (seven-thirty)?* The other pupils answer.

 Make a schedule of your day.

Talk to your friend about it.

- Ask pupils to make a schedule, like the ones in Exercise 3, showing things they do every day.
- Play the model dialog on the cassette for pupils to listen and repeat.
- Pupils talk about their own schedules in pairs.
- Ask pupils questions about their partners' schedules: *What time does (Carlos) get up?* etc.
- Collect pupils' schedules and read details from each. Ask pupils to guess whose they are: *He gets up at a quarter to eight. He rides his bike to school at twenty after eight. (Carlos.)* etc. Pupils take turns reading schedules in the same way.

 Listen and write the words, then find them in the grid.

- Tell pupils they will hear a list of words to write down in their Activity Books.
- Play the cassette, pausing for pupils to write the words.

Tapescript and key

Airplane; bike; bus; cat; cheese; computer; film; studio; fish; football; girl; island; kite; orange; photographs; piano; present; Spain; television; wheel; ball.

- Check the answers with the whole class.
- Pupils find the words in the grid, then check their answers with their partners.

Key

I	C	A	T	C	H	E	A	S	E	P	E
L	A	B	E	O	R	A	N	G	E	H	P
A	F	I	L	M	S	T	U	D	I	O	R
N	O	K	E	P	R	E	S	E	N	T	E
D	O	E	V	U	A	P	I	A	N	O	S
P	T	H	I	T	F	I	S	H	I	G	A
I	B	U	S	E	R	W	L	S	E	R	N
A	A	G	I	R	L	H	A	P	C	A	T
N	L	E	O	M	O	E	N	A	A	P	K
N	L	N	R	O	E	D	I	T	H	I	
O	A	A	I	R	P	L	A	N	E	S	T
W	E	E	L	C	H	E	E	S	E	T	E

The word *cat* appears three times.

 Tell the truth!

- Review the expressions *this morning, last night,* etc. Ask: *What was the date last Thursday? Where were you last month?* etc. Practice the question *When did you last...?* (*When did you last eat a pizza? When did you last clean your room?*) etc.
- Pupils ask and answer the questions in pairs, then write sentences.
- Check the answers with the whole class.

Ending the lesson

Game: When did you last...?

- Ask pupils each to write an activity on a piece of paper e.g. watch television; play a computer game; clean your room; see an elephant. Collect the activities and put them all in a large envelope. Pupils draw out an activity, ask the question: *When did you last (ride a bike)?* and answer it.

Lesson 4

> **Language**
> *Past simple*
>
> **New words and expressions**
> Congratulations!
> winner, judge, poem, poetry
> ago, (four days) later

Beginning the lesson

- Ask pupils to make up sentences about themselves with *usually* and *sometimes*, e.g. *I usually get up at seven o'clock but on Sundays I get up at nine o'clock.*

 ### A surprise for Kate

Listen and point.

- Discuss what is happening in the pictures in L1. Teach the new vocabulary: *Congratulations, winner, judge, ago* and *four days later.*

 Play the cassette. Pupils listen and point to the pictures.

Tapescript and key

Last month Kate read about the photography competition at school. So three weeks ago she took a lot of photographs of her cat, Domino. Four days later, she sent the photographs to the magazine. Last week the judges looked at all the photographs in the competition. They liked Kate's best. And this morning Kate got a letter! She was the winner! She was very excited.

- Read the letter from the judges of the competition with the whole class. Ask questions: *Who's the winner of the competition? What was her photo essay called? When did Kate read about the competition?* etc.

 Play the cassette again. Pupils listen and repeat.

- Pupils talk about the pictures, following the model dialog on the cassette.

 ### Talk about your vacations.

- Ask pupils questions about their vacations: *Where did you go? Did you stay at home? What happened? Did you do anything exciting? What did you see?*

 Play the model dialog on the cassette for pupils to listen and repeat.

 Pupils talk about their vacations in pairs. Help them with new vocabulary.

 ### A poetry competition. Listen and answer the questions.

- Teach the new words *poem* and *poetry*. Tell pupils that they are going to hear about a poetry competition. Read the questions with the whole class.

 Play the cassette. Pupils listen.

 Play the cassette again, pausing for pupils to listen and write answers to the questions.

Tapescript

Don entered a poetry competition last year. He wrote a poem about a wolf. There were three prizes. The first prize was a computer game. The second prize was a football. The third prize was a book. Don won this prize. He chose a book by Roald Dahl, his favorite author.

- Check the answers with the whole class.

Key
1 Last year.
2 A wolf.
3 Three.
4 A computer game.
5 A football.
6 A book.
7 The third prize.

- Discuss competitions: *What kind of competitions do you know about? What are the prizes? Do you like entering competitions?*

Write a poem.

- Discuss the sample poem with the whole class. Ask pupils to say what kind of things (food, clothes, activities) they should use to fill in the gaps.
- Pupils write the words in their poems, then discuss them with their partners.
- Ask pupils to read their poems to the class.

Ending the lesson

- Play the game: *When did you last ...?*

Project idea

- Photo essay: *A day in the life of ...* Pupils can work in pairs or groups to do a photo essay (or draw pictures) showing the life of a person or animal they know.

Assessment activity

- Ask pupils to write sentence answers to the following questions:

1 What time do you usually go to bed?
2 What do you usually have for lunch?
3 Where were you three weeks ago?
4 What time did you go to bed last night?
5 When did you last eat an ice cream cone?

Unit 2   Say cheese!

Lesson 1

Language	New words and expressions
Past simple *Present simple* *make + noun + verb	camera obscura, hole, light, appear, opposite, modern, in the same way, press, button, shutter, let in, lens, film, record, nowadays, powerful, object, magnify, X-ray, gun, trick

* = *new language*

Beginning the lesson

- Discuss cameras and photography in L1. Ask pupils if they own cameras. What kind of photographs do they take? What kind of camera would they like to have?

 Say cheese!

Listen and look.

- Open Pupils' Books at page 6 and ask pupils to tell you what they think the pictures in the Pupils' Book show.

 Listen to the cassette. Pupils follow the text in the Pupils' Book.

- Teach the new vocabulary as you ask questions about the text: *Show me the picture of the camera obscura. Who made it? When did they make it? Where does the picture appear? Tell me about the picture in the camera obscura. (It's upside-down.)* etc.

- Explain that the human eye works in the same way; the image appears upside-down on the retina, but the brain turns the image the right way up again.

Play the cassette again. Pupils listen and read.

- Write questions on the board: *What opens when you press the button on top of the camera? Who took the first photograph? What kind of cameras can look inside people's bodies? What do you need to take secret photographs?*

- Ask pupils to read the passage again and find the answers to the questions. Check the answers with the whole class.

Key

The shutter: Joseph Niepce; X-ray cameras; very small cameras.

AB 5 ex A   **How does it work? Fill in the missing words.**

- Ask pupils to work in pairs to read the passage and find the missing words.

- Check the answers with the whole class.

Key:

A *modern* camera
When you *press* the button *on top of* the camera, the shutter *opens* to let the light in *through* the lens and onto the film. The film *records* the picture.

Ending the lesson

- Play a game of I spy: *(I spy with my little eye, something beginning with ...)*.

Preparation for lesson 2

- Ask pupils to bring photographs (either ones they have taken themselves or ones taken by their family) to class for Exercise 1 in the next lesson.

Lesson 2

Language	New words and expressions
Past simple Did you ...? *Present continuous* * too + adjective * not + adjective + enough * not enough + noun Why?/Because ...	gallery, trailer, still, thumb, clear What did I do wrong?
Materials needed	
pupils' own photographs	

* = *new language*

Beginning the lesson
Opposites games

- Ask pupils, in pairs or groups, to think of words with opposites; e.g. *big* and *small*, *light* and *dark*, *long* and *short*. Then ask them to challenge other pupils to tell them the opposites: *Can you tell*

14

me the opposite of heavy? (Light.). Pupils can work in teams, scoring points for correct questions and answers.

 ## A photo gallery

Bring some of your photos to class. Talk about them to your friend.

 Play the model dialog on the cassette. Pupils listen and repeat.

- Pupils talk about their photos in pairs.
- Ask pupils to tell the rest of the class about their photos.

 ## Ask Uncle Harry

Read and match.

- Teach *too* and *enough*. Ask: *Can you touch the ceiling? (No.) Why not? (It's too high; I'm not tall enough.) Can you walk to ...? (No, it's too far.) Can you lift the cabinet?* etc.
- Read the letter to Uncle Harry with the whole class and teach the new vocabulary: *trailer, still* and *thumb*.
- Pupils read in pairs and match the photos with Uncle Harry's advice.
- Check the answers by asking questions of the whole class: *What's wrong with this picture? Why is the person too small?* etc.

 Play the model dialog on the cassette for pupils to listen and repeat.

- Pupils talk about the photos in pairs.

A photo competition.

- Ask pupils to talk about the photos in pairs, and award them prizes.
- Discuss the pictures with the whole class then ask pupils to write about them. Teach the new word *clear*.
- Check the answers with the whole class.

Key

2 This photo isn't clear because the camera was too far away. (It wasn't near enough).
3 This photo isn't clear because you didn't hold the camera still.
4 This photo isn't clear because you put your thumb in front of the lens.
5 This photo is very good. There's nothing wrong with it.

Ending the lesson

- Pupils can display their photographs on the classroom wall, being careful not to damage

them, and write captions about them. *(This is my birthday party. My brother took this photo last month.)* etc.

Lesson 3

Language	New words and expressions
There is/there are *Prepositions*	behind

Beginning the lesson

- Review prepositions: *in the middle of, next to, on top of, behind, in front of, inside* and *under.* Ask a pupil to move around the classroom: *Please stand in front of the window. Now go behind Maria's chair.* Then ask pupils to give instructions.
- Ask pupils what they can see from different parts of the classroom: *Can you see the door from there? (Yes.) Can you see the wastepaper basket? (No, it's behind the cabinet.) Move to the left. Can you see it now?* etc.

 ## Say cheese!

Song.

 Teach the song in the usual way.

 Play the listening exercise on the cassette, pausing for pupils to listen and find the pictures.

Tapescript and key

Carol: These are some photos of my family. Can you see me? I'm twelve years old and I have red hair and green eyes. My hair is long.

In this photo I'm wearing a white T-shirt. It's a hot, sunny day. My brother is standing next to me. He's eating an ice cream cone. And my sister is building a sand castle. Can you see the ocean? There is a boat on the ocean. Where are we? *(On the beach.)*

In this picture we're having a picnic. There's a lot of food. There are some sandwiches, lots of cake and some bananas. I'm sitting next to my mother. I'm not very happy. My brother is eating a cake. There are two monkeys in this picture. They want the bananas from our picnic! Where are we? *(At the zoo.)*

It's raining in this picture. I'm standing next to my father. My brother is eating a piece of cake. The cake is wet! There are lots of flowers in this picture. We're standing under a tree. Where are we? *(In the country.)*

- Pupils can talk about the photos in pairs.

 Listen and draw.

 Ask pupils to look at the picture of the office. Then play the cassette, pausing for pupils to listen and draw.

Tapescript

There are some flowers in the middle of the table. There are two books on top of the cabinet. There's a picture on the wall. It's next to the clock. There's a mouse inside the cabinet. The woman in the middle is wearing a hat.

- Check the answers with the whole class.

- Ask pupils in pairs to look at the photos from the secret cameras and decide where the cameras were hidden.

- Pupils write their answers in their Activity Books. Check the answers with the whole class.

Key

Camera 1 was on top of the cabinet.
Camera 2 was inside the plant on the table.
Camera 3 was inside the plant on the floor.
Camera 4 was in the woman's hair.

Ending the lesson
- Play the *Opposites game* from lesson 2.

Lesson 4: Activity lesson

Language	New words and expressions
Imperatives	slide, projector, push/pull
Materials needed	
shoe box, flashlight, cardboard, acetate	

Beginning the lesson
- Sing the song: *Say cheese!*

 Can you remember?

How many of these questions can you answer?
- Pupils work in pairs to answer the questions.
- Check the answers with the whole class.

Key

1 Hundreds of years ago.
2 In 1826.
3 We use X-rays to look inside people's bodies.
4 When somebody takes a photo of them.

- Pupils can work in pairs or groups to make true or false statements about cameras and photography to challenge other members of the class.

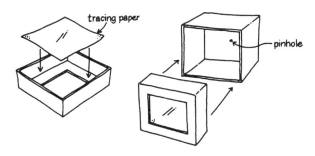 **Make a projector with slides.**

- Read the instructions with the whole class, teaching the new vocabulary.
- Ask questions: *What do you need to make the slides? What do you need to make the projector?*
- Pupils work in pairs or groups to make their projectors and slides.

Ending the lesson
- Pupils can give a slide show for the rest of the class, talking about their pictures, or asking the class to guess what their slides represent.

Project ideas
- Pinhole cameras: Pupils can make their own pinhole cameras, which will show them how cameras work.

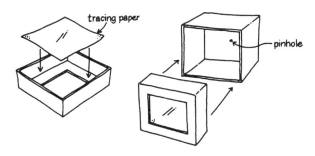

tracing paper

pinhole

- The history of photography: Pupils can research the history of photography, finding out about early cameras, the materials they used to make them and to make photographic plates; examples of old photographs; the first color photos; the different kinds of cameras available today.

Assessment activity
- Ask pupils to write answers to the following questions:

  1 Why can't you touch the classroom ceiling?
  2 Why can't you drive a car?
  3 What can you see through the classroom window?
  4 Is there anybody behind you?
  5 Are you sitting in the middle of the classroom? Where are you sitting?

Unit 3   Action!

Background information
In the story so far, Kate has won a visit to a movie studio as a prize in a photography competition. Sam and Kate's cat, Domino, goes to the movie studio with her.

Lesson 1

Language	New words and expressions
* would like to	fantastic, real, stunt,
* Why don't you...?	some more of, race car,
What does ... do?	sky diving, Be careful,
made of	Action!
	Cut!

* = *new language*

Beginning the lesson

• Ask questions about the story so far: *Where are Kate and Sam? (At a movie studio.) Why? (Because Kate won a prize in a competition.) What was her photo essay called?* etc.

 Action!

Listen and look.

• Open Pupils' Books at page 10 and discuss the story in L1. Ask pupils to tell you what the people in the pictures are doing.

 Listen to the cassette. Pupils follow the story in the Pupils' Book.

• Teach the new vocabulary as you ask questions about the story: *What happens when the director says 'Action'? (They start filming.) Who does the stunts for Marina? (Donna.) What was the window made of?* etc.

 Play the cassette again, pausing for pupils to repeat.

• Pupils read the story again in pairs.

 What does Donna do?

Listen and point.

• Teach the new words: *race car* and *sky diving*.

 Play the cassette, pausing for pupils to listen and point to the movie posters.

Tapescript and key

Kate: I'd like to do stunts like you, Donna.

Sam: So would I. Do you do lots of different things?

Donna: Well, yes. For instance, I drive racing cars. I drive a car in a movie called Wheels.

Kate: I saw that movie! What else do you do?

Donna: Er ... sky diving. I did some sky diving in a movie called Lost in the Skies.

Sam: Do you swim, too?

Donna: Of course. Did you see Atlantic Adventure? I swam in that movie.

Kate: And diving? Do you dive?

Donna: Yes, I dived from the top of the waterfall in Flame of the Forest.

Sam: What else do you do, Donna?

Donna: Oh, lots of things. I ride horses. I rode a horse in Tales of the West. And I ski. I skied in a movie called Avalanche!

Kate: Is it very dangerous?

Donna: Sometimes. We must always be very careful.

• Ask questions about Donna: *What did she do in Flame of the Forest? (She dived from the top of a waterfall.)* etc.

 Play the model dialog on the cassette for pupils to listen and repeat.

• Pupils talk about Donna in pairs.

Ending the lesson

• Ask pupils in pairs to role play an interview between a stunt man or woman and a movie director: *Can you swim? (Yes.) Can you jump from a high building?* etc.

Preparation for Lesson 2

• Drawing materials.

Lesson 2

Language	New words and expressions
I'd like to ...	stunt artist, join, gymnastics,
Why don't you ...?	club, race, school sports,
	movie-making, enormous
Materials needed	
drawing materials	

Beginning the lesson

- Ask the pupils about sports and activities they do: *Do you do sky diving? Do you do underwater swimming? Do you do photography?* etc. Pupils can ask questions themselves.

 Why don't you ...?

Read and match.

- Teach the language: *I'd like to (be a stunt artist). Why don't you (do it)? stunt artist, join, gymnastics, club, race, school sports, movie making* and *enormous*.

- Pupils work in pairs to match the sentences and the suggestions.

- Check the answers by reading the sentences with the whole class.

  Key:

  I'd like to be a stunt artist. (Why don't you join a gymnastics club?)
  I'd like to win a race in the school sports. (Why don't you have a jog every day?)
  I'd like to find out about movie-making. (Why don't you borrow a book about it from the library?)
  I'd like to buy my friend an enormous birthday cake. (Why don't you make one?)

- Ask pupils to talk to their partners about what they would like or love to do. Pupils could draw pictures showing themselves in an ideal situation and then describe it to their partners: *I'd love to have a fast car. I'd like to drive it through (town)* etc.

- Ask pupils about their own and their partners' ambitions: *What would Maria like to do? What would she like to wear?*

 Which prize would you choose? Write a sentence about what you would like to do.

- Ask pupils to talk about the prizes in the competition in pairs: *What would you like to do? I'd like to (drive a race car.)*

- Pupils write what they would like to do in their Activity Books. Ask questions with the whole class: *Would you like to drive a race car, Maria? (No, I wouldn't.) What would you like to do?* etc.

- Pupils ask other members of the class what they would like to do (they can only choose one prize each) and fill in the chart.

 Read and match.

- Ask pupils to read and match the sentences and the suggestions.

- Check the answers with the whole class.

  Key

  2d 3b 4f 5c 6a

Ending the lesson

- Ask questions about the chart in exercise A of the Activity Book: *How many people in the class would like to visit the pyramids?* etc.

Lesson 3

Language	New words and expressions
Imperatives	Look out!
mustn't	no entry, silence, in shape, healthy, lemonade, housework

Beginning the lesson

- Ask pupils to make suggestions using *Why don't you ...? Say: I'm hungry. (Why don't you have some cake?) I'm cold. (Why don't you close the window?) I'd love to see a kangaroo. (Why don't you go to the zoo?)* etc.

 Warning signs

Listen and point. Then listen and repeat.

- Teach the new words: *Look out! No entry* and *silence*.

 Play the cassette, pausing for pupils to listen and point to the signs.

  Tapescript and key

  Narrator: One.
  Boy: Look out! Don't go in there!
  Girl: Why? What's the matter?
  Boy: There's a sign. It says "No entry".
  Narrator: Two
  Girl: Shh! Don't talk!
  Boy: Why not?
  Girl: Look at the sign. It says "Silence".
  Narrator: Three.
  Boy: Look out! Don't touch!
  Girl: Why?
  Boy: Look at the sign! It says "Do not touch". It's dangerous.
  Narrator: Four.
  Girl: You mustn't smoke here.
  Man: What?
  Girl: See the sign? It means "No smoking".

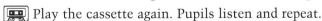 Play the cassette again. Pupils listen and repeat.

- Ask pupils where they can see signs like these (e.g. Danger signs where construction work is going on; No smoking in kitchens).

Ask and answer the questions with a friend.

- Teach *in shape, healthy, lemonade* and *housework*. Pupils ask and answer the questions in pairs.

- Pupils list the good and bad things to do in their Activity Books. Check the answers with the whole class.

Key

Eat lots of fruit and vegetables.	Don't eat lots of candy.
Drink lots of water.	Don't drink lots of lemonade.
Do exercises every day.	Don't go to bed late.
Play football or tennis.	Don't play lots of computer games.
Go swimming.	
Ride a bike.	Don't watch lots of TV.
Help with the housework.	

 Pupils write about what they do and don't do in their Activity Books, e.g. *I eat lots of vegetables but I don't eat lots of candy.*

Ending the lesson

- Ask pupils to continue thinking of other ways to stay in shape and healthy in pairs. Discuss their answers with the whole class.

Lesson 4

Language	New words and expressions
can/can't	balance, hoop, rescue, scene, lead
need	wedding, husband, blonde, hate

Beginning the lesson

- Discuss in L1 animals pupils have seen in movies or on television. What kind of things can the animals do?

 Animal stars

Read and find the best dog for the movie part.

- Teach the new words b*alance, hoop, rescue, scene* and *lead*.

- Ask pupils in pairs to read the description of what the dog in the movie has to do, and find the best dog for the part.

- Check the answers by asking questions with the whole class. *Can Bilbo swim? (No.) Which dog can swim? (Murphy.) Do they need a dog who can swim? (No.)* etc. *What do they need? (A dog who can climb a ladder; jump over a wall; open a door with its nose.)*

Key

The right dog for the part is Sparky.

- Pupils can practice interviewing the dogs' owners in pairs.

  A: What's your dog's name?
  B: Bilbo.
  A: How old is he?
  B: Two years old.
  A: Can he swim?
  B: Yes.

 Listen and write the numbers.

- Teach the new words: *wedding, husband, blonde* and *hate.*

- Play the cassette, pausing for pupils to listen and write the numbers in the boxes.

Tapescript

Gloria: Look, this is a photo of my wedding. This is my new husband, Gary. Do you like my dress?

Sharon: Yes, it's lovely! I like this woman's hat, with the flowers.

Gloria: That's my mother. And that's my father – he's the bald man. He's talking to my sister.

Sharon: Who's the woman with the long dark hair?

Gloria: Oh, that's Elvira Smart – she's very famous. She's my friend. Can you see my brother? He's eating a sandwich – he's always eating.

Sharon: I like the little dog.

Gloria: Yes, that's Fou Fou – my aunt never goes out without her dog. Can you guess which is my grandmother?

Sharon: Your grandmother! How old is she?

Gloria: She's eight-five but she looks younger. That's her. She's reading a book. And that's my grandfather, talking to Elvira. He has a cup of coffee in his hand.

- Check the answers with the whole class.

- Pupils can continue talking about the picture in pairs: *Who's that? (That's Gloria's husband.)* etc.

Movie tricks. What are they made of? Read and match.

- Discuss in L1 the way things in movies can be made of different materials so that actors and stunt artists don't get hurt.

- Ask pupils to read and match in pairs.

- Check the answers with the whole class by asking questions: *What are windows in movies made of? (Sugar.)* etc.

Key

2 Windows are made of sugar.
3 Monsters are made of rubber.
4 Furniture is made of paper.
5 Buildings are made of wood.

Ending the lesson

• Ask pupils in groups, or as a whole class, to make up a story for an adventure movie and then role play interviews with stunt artists and animal owners for it: *Can you drive a race car? Can your horse swim across a river?* etc.

Project idea

• Keep in shape and healthy: Pupils can find out more about keeping in shape and healthy and write a booklet or make posters advising people what to do.

Assessment activity

• Ask pupils to write sentence answers to the following questions:

1 What are monsters in movies made of?
2 What sport would you like to do?
3 What do you do to keep in shape and healthy?
4 What does "no entry" mean?
5 Where would you like to go on vacation?

Language review 1

Lesson 1

Language	New words and expressions
Simple present *Simple past*	tuba

Beginning the lesson

- Ask pupils to tell you things they do every day, every week, every weekend, etc. Then ask them about the past; yesterday, last week, last weekend, etc.

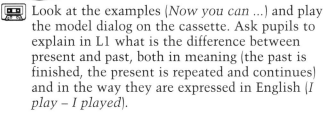 **Present and past tenses**

- Look at the examples (*Now you can ...*) and play the model dialog on the cassette. Ask pupils to explain in L1 what is the difference between present and past, both in meaning (the past is finished, the present is repeated and continues) and in the way they are expressed in English (*I play – I played*).

- Look at the file cards with the class. Ask them to try to think of other verbs that end in *-ed* in the past tense (*watch, talk, listen, show, like, visit, work*). Ask pupils to think of other verbs that have irregular endings in the past tense (*saw, went, came, made, had, gave*, etc.).

PB 14 Things to do

- Ask pupils to think about things they do now which they didn't do last year, and things they did last year which they don't do now. For example, games they play, pop stars they like, things they eat. Pupils talk about these in pairs and make sentences: *I play basketball now. I didn't play basketball last year. I watched cartoons on TV last year. I don't watch them now.*

- Pupils tell the class about themselves and their partners. Compare pupils' answers: *How many people didn't like pizza last year?*

Ending the lesson

- Discuss how people change as they grow older. Ask pupils to tell you what their younger brothers and sisters or their parents did in the past and what they do now.

Preparation for lesson 2

- Ask pupils to bring a small empty box (e.g. the kind that contains food) to class to make a container for their file cards. Show them an example of the kind of thing you mean.

Lesson 2

Language	New words and expressions
Simple past *Simple present*	file card, file box
Materials needed	
boxes, scissors, paint, cardboard	

Beginning the lesson

- Review simple past and simple present by asking questions: *What did you watch on TV yesterday? Did you watch the news? Do you watch the news every day?*

 Make a box for your language file cards.

- Look at the instructions with the class. Pupils follow the instructions to make their boxes, then measure them and cut out file cards to fit the boxes.

 Things to do

- Pupils copy the cards in the Pupils' Book, choosing a different verb instead of *play*, and put them in their language boxes.

 Complete the table of past tense verbs.

- Ask pupils to fill in the missing verbs in the table. Check the answers with the whole class.

Key

verb	past	verb	past	verb	past
see	saw	go	went	take	took
do	did	come	came	make	made
have	had	eat	ate	say	said

- Pupils can add to this table and make cards for their language files.

Listen and check the correct pictures.

- Ask pupils to look at the pictures and identify the things in them.

 Play the cassette. Pupils listen and check the correct pictures.

Tapescript and key

- What did Sharon do at the beach? Listen and check the correct pictures.

  Boy: Where did you go on Saturday, Sharon?
  Sharon: I went to the beach. It was great!
  Boy: What did you do?
  Sharon: Well, all kinds of things. I played table tennis.
  Boy: On the beach?
  Sharon: Yeah, why not? then ... um ... I ate a burger. Then I went fishing.
  Boy: Did you catch anything?
  Sharon: Well ... I caught a starfish. Then I bought this hat. Do you like it?
  Boy: Hm. Isn't it rather big?
  Sharon: Yes. I love it. I wore it with my pink shorts on the beach.
  Boy: Did anything else happen?
  Sharon: Oh yes. I lost one of my shoes.
  Boy: Oh no!

 Ask pupils to read the questions. Play the cassette again for pupils to listen to the past tense verbs.

- Pupils write answers to the questions and check them with their partners. Check the answers with the whole class.

  Key

  1 She bought a big hat.
  2 She ate a burger.
  3 She played table tennis.
  4 She caught a starfish.
  5 She lost a shoe.

Ending the lesson

Game: We went to the beach.

- The first player says: *We went to the beach and I ate an apple.* The second player adds an item to the list: *We went to the beach. Maria ate an apple and I played basketball.* Continue around the class, each player adding an activity to the list. The nouns can be in alphabetical order, e.g. *apple, basketball, cola,* etc., though this will make the game more difficult.

Lesson 3

Language	New words and expressions
Simple past	encyclopedia, volume

Beginning the lesson

- Tell pupils that they are going to read about the history of the movies. Ask them what tense (past or present) they expect the information to be written in.

PB 15 **Skills review 1: Reading**

- Ask pupils to tell you where they would look for information for a project (in the library, in an encyclopedia, etc.).

- Read the questions with the class. Ask if they know or can guess the answers to any of the questions.

- Ask pupils to look for the answers in the passage, working in pairs, and noting their answers. Tell them to work as quickly as possible. Remind them to ignore the information they do not need.

- Check the answers with the class.

  Key

  William Dickson; the Lumiere brothers; very short; between 1908 and 1918; The Jazz Singer.

- Ask pupils to look at the passage again and note any words they did not know (e.g. kinetoscope, nickelodeon). Did they need these words to answer the questions? Explain that often when they are looking for information, it doesn't matter if they don't understand every word.

- Ask pupils to work through the *Things to do* section in pairs. Check the answers with the whole class.

  Key

  1 K – O
  2 Ask pairs of pupils to ask the class their questions e.g. Where was the first motion picture show?
  3 invented; looked; saw; was; projected; began; showed; opened; became

Ending the lesson

- Ask pupils to imagine they were doing a project about the history of the movies in their country. What questions would they ask? e.g. When did the first movie theater open? Where was it? Who made the first movie? Where was the first studio? Ask them how they would find out the information they needed.

Optional Lesson 4

Beginning the lesson

- Ask pupils to tell you about the things they do every day. This could be done as a statistical survey to find out, for instance, how far they walk every day, how long they spend on different activities or how much of different kinds of food they eat.

More practice with simple present and simple past

1 Pupils work in pairs to list the present and past tense verbs on page 6 of the Pupils' Book.

2 Look at Domino's day on page 3 of the Pupils' Book. Ask pupils to write it out as *What Domino did yesterday* in the past tense.

3 Ask pupils to interview each other about what they did at the weekend. Pupils can report their partners' activities to the class.

Ending the lesson

- Play the game *We went to the beach* from Unit 1, lesson 2.

Unit 4   My favorite movies

Lesson 1

Language	New words and expressions
What kind of ...?	movie, cine camera,
would like to + verb	every minute, quickly,
Simple present	machine, project, screen,
seem to + verb	need (something) to,
	actor, actress, director,
	camera operator,
	producer, sound recordist

Beginning the lesson

- Ask the questions: *What kind of movies do you like? (Cartoons, adventure movies, comedies, horror movies, science fiction.)* Teach the expression: *I like to see (cartoons). What's your favorite movie? Who's your favorite movie star?*

 Which movies are these people going to see?

Read and match.

- Ask pupils to tell you the names of the movies in the photos *(Jurassic Park, The Flintstones and Home Alone 2).*

- Ask pupils to read about the kind of movies Alison, Peter and Scott like, and find the movies they are going to see.

  Key

  Alison is going to see Jurassic Park.
  Peter is going to see The Flintstones.
  Scott is going to see Home Alone 2.

 How do you make a movie?

- Ask pupils to look at the picture from a movie set. Explain that you need a lot of different people to make a movie. Ask the pupils who they think the people are and what they do. Teach the words *actor/actress, producer, director, camera operator* and *sound recordist.*

 Who are they?

Listen and point.

 Play the cassette, pausing for pupils to listen and point to the people in the picture.

Tapescript and key

Girl: What are all these people doing?
Boy: They're making a movie. Look, there are three actors in the middle.
Girl: Oh yes, I see. There's a woman and two men. But who are all the other people?
Boy: Well, can you see the camera?
Girl: Yes.
Boy: Well, the person behind the camera is the camera operator.
Girl: Where's the director?
Boy: There she is, sitting in the middle, in front of the actors. She's telling them all what to do.
Girl: Is that microphone recording the sound?
Boy: Yes, and the person holding the microphone is the sound recordist.
Girl: Is the producer there?
Boy: Yes, he is. There he is, standing next to the sound recordist. He's wearing a red sweater.

- Check the answers by asking the questions to the whole class: *Who's this? Where's the camera operator?* etc.

 Play the model dialog on the cassette for pupils to listen and repeat. Pupils talk about the picture in pairs.

 Fill in the gaps with the correct people.

- The exercise talks about all the people needed to make a movie. Pupils read the passage in pairs and fit the missing people into the gaps, referring to page 17 of the Pupils' Book.

- Check the answers with the whole class.

  Key

  The *producer* finds the money to make the movie. He is the boss. The *director* tells everyone what to do. The *camera operator* operates the cine-camera. The *actresses* and *actors* act in front of the cameras.

Ending the lesson

- Pupils talk in pairs about the people who make films: *What does the producer do? He finds the money to make the movie* etc.

Lesson 2

Language	New words and expressions
Would you like to...?	start + ing
Past simple	the Atlantic
How long does it take?	

Beginning the lesson

- Ask pupils: *Would you like to work in movies? What would you like to be? (A producer, an actor)* etc. *What kind of movies would you like to make?*

 ## A young actress

- Ask pupils to work in pairs to suggest questions to ask the actress and write them down.

- Ask pupils to read their questions to the class.

 Play the cassette. Pupils listen and see if Tamara answers their questions.

Tapescript

Narrator: Tamara is twelve years old. She's an actress. Listen to this interview with her. Does she answer your questions?

Interviewer: When did you become an actress?

Tamara: Um, well I've been acting all my life in school shows but I really seriously started acting last year.

Interviewer: Do you like acting?

Tamara: Yes. I love it.

Interviewer: Do you go to school?

Tamara: Yes. I go to a special school. We do normal lessons in the morning and dance and drama in the afternoon.

Interviewer: Do you make lots of movies?

Tamara: Well, quite a few.

Interviewer: Is acting difficult?

Tamara: Well, acting in movies can be difficult, but acting in the theater isn't.

Interviewer: What's your favorite movie?

Tamara: My favorite movie must be *Forever Young.*

Interviewer: And who's your favorite movie star?

Tamara: Mel Gibson.

- Ask questions about the interview with the whole class.

 ## Listen to Kate's interview with Marina Wilson. Can you write Kate's questions?

- Ask pupils to work in pairs to guess what the questions are in the interview.

 Play the cassette, pausing for pupils to write the questions.

Tapescript and key

Kate: Marina, can I ask you some questions about your life?

Marina: Yes, of course.

Kate: What kind of movies do you like?

Marina: I like all kinds of movies, but I never miss adventure movies.

Kate: When did you start acting?

Marina: I started acting when I was ten years old.

Kate: Do you have any pets?

Marina: Yes, I have two cats and a dog.

Kate: How do you keep in shape?

Marina: I usually run in the park every morning, and I go swimming sometimes.

Kate: And what will your next movie be?

Marina: My next movie will be a science fiction movie.

Play the cassette again. Pupils listen and repeat.

Working in pairs, pupils write questions for their favorite movie stars.

 ## How long do these things take? Read and choose the right answer.

- Teach and practice questions with *How long does it take? How long does it take you to come to school? How long does it take you to eat your breakfast?* etc.

- Pupils answer the questions in pairs.

Key

It takes Concorde five hours to cross the Atlantic.
It takes the moon twenty-four hours to travel around the earth.
It takes the earth a year to travel around the sun.
It takes a cheetah six minutes to run ten kilometers.

- Pupils ask and answer questions about themselves in pairs, then write sentences in their Activity Books.

Ending the lesson

- Ask pupils to tell the class about the best movies they have seen.

Preparation for lesson 3

- Materials for making sound effects: shoes (light and heavy); watering can and bowl; cellophane; rice and aluminum pie pan; large sheet of cardboard or aluminum.

Lesson 3

Language	New words and expressions
It sounds like ... What does it sound like?	fire, rainstorm, thunderstorm, soldier, march, cellophane, coconut shell, tank, hoof, sound effect

Materials needed

shoes (light and heavy); watering can and bowl; cellophane; rice and aluminium pie pan; large sheet of cardboard or aluminium

Beginning the lesson

• Review *What does ... taste like? What does ... smell like?* Ask questions: *What does chocolate taste like?* etc. Pupils ask questions themselves.

 Sound effects

What does it sound like? Listen and say.

• Teach the new vocabulary: *sound effect. What does it sound like? It sounds like ... fire, rainstorm, thunderstorm, soldier and march.*

 Play the cassette. Pupils listen and point to the pictures.

Tapescript

1 *Someone swimming.*
2 *A child running.*
3 *A soldier marching.*
4 *A forest fire.*
5 *A rainstorm.*
6 *A thunderstorm.*

 Play the model dialog on the cassette. Pupils listen and repeat.

 Play the cassette again. Pupils ask and answer questions about the sounds: *What does this sound like? It sounds like someone swimming*, etc.

• Use the materials for making sound effects. Demonstrate or ask pupils to demonstrate how you can make the sound of someone swimming by splashing water in a bowl; the sound of feet with different kinds of shoes; the sound of rain with a watering can or by dropping rice on an aluminum pie pan; the sound of thunder by shaking a large sheet of cardboard or aluminum; the sound of a fire by crumpling cellophane.

• Ask pupils to ask and answer questions while making the sounds: *What does this sound like? It sounds like (fire)*, etc.

 How can you make the sound effects? Read and match.

• Teach the new words *coconut shell* and *tank*.

• Pupils read and match the sound effects.

Key

1 You can use paper to make the sound of fire.
2 You can use a watering can to make the sound of rain.
3 You can use a tank of water to make the sound of splashing.
4 You can use boots and shoes to make the sound of footsteps.
5 You can use coconut shells to make the sound of horses' feet.

 Make a soundtrack

• Discuss what is happening in the pictures with the whole class.

• In pairs or groups, pupils decide which sound effects they will need for each picture.

 Play the model dialog on the cassette. Pupils listen and repeat, then ask and answer questions about the pictures.

• Ask questions with the whole class.

Ending the lesson

• Guess the sound effect: Pupils use the materials, or other things around the classroom for sound effects. One group of pupils makes a sound effect, and the others have to say what it sounds like and how they made it: *What does this sound like? (Rain.) How did we make it? (By dropping rice on a pan.).*

Preparation for lesson 4

• Materials for sound effects, a microphone and blank cassette tape.

Lesson 4

Language	New words and expressions
How long does it take? number + times	the most popular ... ever produce, earn, the most money

Materials needed

materials for sound effects, blank cassette, microphone for cassette player

Beginning the lesson

• Ask pupils questions about their favorite movies. *What kind of movies do you like? Which is the best movie you ever saw? When did you see it? Who's your favorite movie star?*

Are you crazy about movies?

Answer the questions with your friend.

- Read the questions with the whole class, teaching the new vocabulary: *Fifteen times. The most popular movie ever, produce, earn, the most money.*
- Pupils answer the questions in pairs.
- Check pupils' answers with the whole class.

  Key

  1 b
  2 a (at least!)
  3 b
  4 a
  5 a

- Ask questions: *Which country produced 900 movies every year? (India.)* etc.

 Read the story.

- Read the story with the whole class, asking pupils to suggest suitable sound effects.
- Pupils read the story in pairs or groups, making appropriate sound effects.
- Help pupils record the story, with their sound effects.

Ending the lesson

- Play the recording for the whole class to listen to.

Project ideas

- Movie project: Pupils can find out about a movie or movies. (When was it made? Where was it made? Who was the director? Who were the stars? etc.). Or they could find out about the history of movie making in their own country.
- Radio scripts: Pupils can research and write their own radio dramas/documentaries incorporating sound effects. Help them choose themes e.g. making a movie, exciting outdoor sports, their hobbies, what their parents do for a living, environmental projects. They could cast and produce them in teams playing director, researcher, producer, actors, sound recordist, etc., and record them on cassette.
- Sound effects library: help pupils draw up a list of stock sound effects. They can then research ways of making them and record them. Pupils could then have a competition for a) the best sound effect and b) the most correct guesses of other people's sound effects.

Assessment activity

- Ask pupils to write questions for the following answers:

  1 She records the voices and the sound effects.
  2 It takes fifteen minutes.
  3 I like science fiction movies.
  4 By shaking a big piece of cardboard.
  5 It sounds like a rainstorm.

Unit 5   On location

Background information

Kate and Sam are in Mexico. They have been invited to appear in an adventure movie, "Jake the Pirate" with the movie star, Marina Wilson.

Lesson 1

Language	New words and expressions
going to	on location, shoot, battle, costume, soldiers, attack, escape, cannon, fire

Beginning the lesson

- Discuss movies with the class. *Would they like to be in a movie? What kind of movie would they like to be in? What kind of clothes would they like to wear in a movie?*

PB 20 On location

Listen and look.

- Open Pupils' Books at page 20 and discuss the story in L1. Ask pupils to tell you what the characters in the pictures are doing.
- Listen to the cassette. Pupils follow the story in the Pupils' Book.
- Teach the new vocabulary: *on location, shoot, battle, costume, soldiers, attack, escape, cannon, fire.*
- Play the cassette again, pausing for pupils to repeat.
- Pupils read the story again in pairs.

PB 21 ex 1 What are they going to do?

- Play the model dialog on the cassette. Pupils listen and repeat.
- Ask pupils to work in pairs to read the story again and find out what the people in the picture are doing.
- Check the answers by asking questions: *Who can you see in picture 1? What are they going to do?*

Key

1 The pirates are going to fire the cannon.
2 The soldiers are going to attack from the shore.
3 Jake Jones is going to fight the soldiers.
4 Kate and Sam are going to watch the battle from behind a rock.
5 Marina is going to escape from the ship.

AB 16 ex A Find these things in the picture.

- Ask pupils to look at the picture and write the numbers beside the things in the picture.
- Check the answers with the class.

Ending the lesson

- Ask questions about the story: *Who do you think is going to win the battle? What's Marina going to do next? What's the director going to do?* etc.

Lesson 2

Language	New words and expressions
* would rather	special

* = *new language*

Beginning the lesson

- Ask questions with *Would you like ...?* (*Would you like to be in a movie? Would you like to go to Africa? Would you like to have an apple?* etc.). Ask pupils to think of similar questions to ask each other.

PB 22 ex 2 Lisa's special day

Listen and point.

- Teach *would rather*. Give pupils things to choose: *Would you like a blue pen or a red one? (I'd rather have ...).*
- Look at the pictures with the class and ask them to identify the objects and activities. Play the cassette. Pupils listen and point.
- Check the answers by asking the questions to the whole class. *Where would Lisa rather go?* (to an amusement park) etc.

Tapescript and key

Scott: Imagine it's your special day, Lisa. Would you like to go to the beach?
Lisa: I'd rather go to an amusement park.
Scott: What would you like to wear? The blue T-shirt?
Lisa: Mm ... No, I'd rather wear the green one.
Scott: Would you like to ride on a horse?
Lisa: Yes, but I'd rather ride on an elephant.
Scott: I'd like to try water skiing. Would you?
Lisa: I'd rather try sailing.
Scott: Would you like to see an adventure movie?

Lisa: I'd rather see a cartoon.
Scott: Which would you rather meet, a movie star or a pop star?
Lisa: I'd rather meet my favorite pop star.

 Play the cassette again, pausing for pupils to listen and repeat.

 ### What would you like to do on a special day?

Talk to your friends.

 Play the model dialog on the cassette. Pupils listen and repeat.

- Pupils talk about their own plans for a special day in pairs or groups. Ask questions with the whole class. (*Who would like to go to the beach? Who'd rather go to the mountains?* etc.)

 ### Write answers to the questions using *I'd rather ...*

- Do the first question orally with the class. Then ask pupils to write their own answers to the questions in their Activity Books.
- Ask pupils to ask and answer the questions in pairs. Check the answers with the whole class.

Ending the lesson

Game: I'd rather ...

- Divide the class into teams. Ask pupils each to write a question beginning *Would you like to ...?* e.g. *... play tennis; go to Italy; learn to ski; have a cup of coffee.* Collect the questions and put them all in a large envelope. Pupils draw out a question and ask a member of another team *Would you like to (play tennis)?* The person asked answers *I'd rather (play basketball).* The question should be answered within a time limit to win a point for the player's team.

Lesson 3

Language	New words and expressions
Present continuous going to	dream

Beginning the lesson

- Teach the new word *dream*. Ask pupils what the people in the pictures on page 23 of the Pupils' Book are dreaming. Ask pupils if they have similar dreams.

 ### Dreams

Song.

- Teach the song in the usual way.

 ### What's your dream?

Draw a picture of your dream and talk about it with your friends.

 Play the model dialog on the cassette for pupils to listen and repeat.

- Ask pupils to draw pictures of their own dreams, then describe them, working in pairs or groups.

 ### What are they going to do? Write about the pictures.

- Ask pupils to work in pairs to describe what the people in the pictures are going to do and then write the answers in their Activity Books.
- Check the answers with the whole class.

  Key

  1 They're going to make a movie.
  2 She's going to catch a bus.
  3 He's going to open the window.
  4 They're going to go skiing.
  5 He's going to eat an apple.
  6 He's going to go fishing.

Ending the lesson

- Ask pupils to mime things they dream of doing for the rest of the class to guess.

Lesson 4

Language
going to
I'd like to ...
I'd rather ...

Beginning the lesson

- Sing the song *Dreams.*

 ### What's Don going to do? Listen and circle the words that are wrong.

- Ask pupils to read about Don's birthday plans.

 Play the cassette. Pupils to listen and circle the words that are wrong in the Activity Book.

  Tapescript and key

  It's my birthday next week and my parents are going to take me to a restaurant. I'm going to invite my friends Joe and Sally to come with us. We're going to arrive there at seven o'clock. We're going to have pizzas to eat. I think there's going to be a birthday cake. Then we're going to see a movie.

- Check the answers with the whole class.

 Play the cassette again for pupils to make notes of what Don really said. In pairs, pupils check their answers.

 What would you like to do? Talk to your friend and then write sentences.

- Discuss the activities going on in the movie studio in the picture. Ask pupils to work in pairs to discuss what they would like to do if they had two hours at a movie studio.

- Ask pupils to write down their answers *We'd like to ... them ...* etc.

- Check pupils' answers with the whole class. Ask questions: *Would you like to visit the land of dinosaurs? No. We'd rather (make a video)* etc.

- Pupils can continue asking similar questions in groups.

Ending the lesson

- Play the game: *I'd rather ...* from Lesson 2.

Project idea

- Pupils could find out more about what happens when a movie crew goes on location.

Assessment activity

- Ask pupils to write answers to the following questions.

1 What are you going to do next Saturday?
2 Would you like to be a movie director?
3 Which would you rather do, play a computer game or watch a video?
4 Where would you like to go for your vacation?
5 Would you like to have fish for dinner?

Unit 6   A famous pirate

Background information

Pirates in the Caribbean in the 17th and 18th centuries have inspired a lot of stories and movies. The pirates were mostly European adventurers tempted by the rich Spanish treasure ships returning to Spain from the New World. Most real-life pirates were not notably successful and did not acquire huge amounts of treasure.

A map of the world would be helpful so that pupils can find the places mentioned in this unit.

Lesson 1

Language	New words and expressions
Simple past	treasure, sword, coin, flag, chest, gun, belt, coast, fierce, bury, kill

Beginning the lesson

• Ask pupils about the movie that Kate and Sam are appearing in. *What's its name? What is it about? What kind of things happen in it?*

 PB 24 A famous pirate

Listen and look.

• Open Pupils' Books at page 24 and read the introduction to the story. Teach the words in the box, and ask pupils to find the things in the pictures on pages 24 and 25 of the Pupils' Book.

• Discuss the pictures on page 24 in L1. Ask pupils to tell you what they think is happening in the pictures.

• Listen to the cassette. Pupils follow the text in the Pupils' Book.

• Teach the new vocabulary: *gun, belt, coast, fierce, bury* and *kill.*

• Play the cassette again, pausing for pupils to repeat.

 PB 25 ex 1 Ask three questions

• Ask pupils to read the model questions and answer them. Play the model dialog on the cassette. Pupils listen and repeat.

• Pupils ask three questions with *who* and ask their partners. Then ask three questions with *where.*

• Check the answers with the whole class.

 AB 19 ex A Find the missing words in the treasure chest.

• Ask pupils to work in pairs to guess the words that are missing and find them in the treasure chest.

• Check the answers with the class.

Key

My name is Blackbeard. I'm a famous pirate. I'm very fierce. I wear lots of swords and guns. I steal jewels and coins and bury my treasure on islands in the Caribbean. Can you find the missing words in the treasure chest?

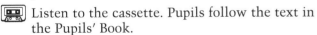

T	C	A	T	O	A	I	N
R	O	H	B	U	R	Y	K
E	I	X	E	Z	Q	F	V
A	N	R	A	S	H	I	P
S	P	I	R	A	T	E	G
U	J	Q	D	L	B	R	U
R	S	W	O	R	D	C	N
E	K	Z	J	E	W	E	L

Ending the lesson

• Ask pupils, with books closed, to remember as many facts as they can about Blackbeard e.g. He was very fierce. He carried lots of guns, swords and knives. A British captain killed him in 1718.

Lesson 2

Language
Simple past
because
too

Beginning the lesson

• Ask questions about Blackbeard: *What did he look like? What was his real name? Where did he attack the treasure ships?*

Read about Blackbeard. Then match the two parts of the sentences from A and B.

- Ask pupils to match the sentences then check their answers in pairs.

- Check the answers orally with the whole class.

  Key

  2 He attacked ships off the American coast.
  3 He stole gold and jewels from the treasure ships.
  4 He buried his treasure on small islands in the West Indies.
  5 A British captain put Blackbeard's head on the front of his ship.

 Blackbeard's treasure

Listen to Blackbeard and his men. Look at the map and find the treasure.

- Ask pupils to look at the map and tell you what they can see on it. Ask them to see if they can find a good place for Blackbeard to hide his treasure.

 Play the cassette. Pupils listen and find the places on the map.

  Tapescript and key

Pirate:	Let's bury it here on the beach, Captain!
Blackbeard:	No, it's too hot here. The treasure will melt!
Pirate:	Let's bury it here then, under this bridge.
Blackbeard:	No, it's too dangerous. Look at those crocodiles!
Pirate:	Let's bury it here in this cave.
Blackbeard:	No, it's too wet. Look at all this water. Let's hide it up there on top of that mountain.
Pirate:	No – we can't carry it up there! It's too heavy!
Pirate:	Let's hide it here.
Blackbeard:	No, there are too many monkeys. They'll find it.
Pirate:	Let's hide it here!
Blackbeard:	No, there are too many people. They'll see us.
Pirate:	There – that's the place! We'll hide it there in that cave!
Pirates:	Thank goodness!

 Play the model dialog on the cassette. Pupils listen and repeat.

- Check the answers by asking questions about the places on the map to the whole class: *Did they bury the treasure here? No, they didn't because it was too hot.*

Ending the lesson

Game: Where's the treasure?

- Ask pupils, working in groups to think of a place in or near their school to hide some treasure. The other groups must ask questions to find out where the imaginary treasure is hidden: *Is it in the river? Is it in the park?* etc.

Lesson 3

Language	New words and expressions
Simple past tense	fleet, log book, journey
Present continuous	join, hang

Beginning the lesson

- Look at the picture of the ships on page 26 of the Pupils' Book with the class. Ask: *Are they different from ships today? Did they go very fast? What did the men on the ships do?* etc.

 Treasure ships

 Play the cassette. Pupils listen and read. Teach the new words: *fleet, log book* and *journey*.

 Play the model dialog for pupils to listen and repeat. Pupils read the log book page again and ask the answer questions. Check the answers with the class.

- Ask pupils to write about the treasure ships in the past tense. Do the first few sentences orally with the class. Then ask pupils to work in pairs to write about the treasure ships.

- Check the answers with the class.

  Key

  Every year from 1560 to 1780 a fleet of ships left Seville. They sailed across the Atlantic Ocean to the New World. They took clothes, food and furniture to the Spanish people who lived in the West Indies and in Veracruz on the Mexican coast. They brought back gold and silver for their king. The journey back to Spain was very dangerous because there were many British and French pirates. they wanted to steal their treasure.

- Ask questions about the treasure ships: *Which ocean did they sail across? How many ships left Seville? Where is Seville?* etc.

Listen to a true story about two pirates.

Check true or false.

- Look at the picture with the class. Ask them what they think the story is going to be about. Teach the new words: *join* and *hang*.

 Play the cassette, pausing for pupils to check true or false.

Tapescript

Not all pirates were men. Anne Bonney, an English woman, joined the crew of Jack Rackham's pirate ship in the West Indies. She fought and killed many men.

Mary Reade, an English woman, wore men's clothes and worked on the King's ships for many years. Nobody knew she was a woman. Rackham, the pirate, attacked Mary's ship in the West Indies. Mary joined his crew and became a pirate too. Years later the police found Rackham's ship. The men hid at the bottom of the ship, but the women fought fiercely. The police hanged the men and the women watched. Anne Bonney said, "They died because they didn't fight like men".

 Play the cassette again for pupils to check their answers. Then check the answers with the whole class.

Key

1 false **2** true **3** true **4** false **5** true **6** false **7** true

 Write the past tense form of these verbs.

- Pupils write the past tense form of the verbs and check their answers with their partners.
- Check the answers with the whole class.

Key

1 attacked **2** buried **3** cut **4** killed **5** left **6** wore **7** became **8** stole **9** took

Ending the lesson

- Ask questions about the story of the women pirates: *What were the names of the women pirates? Who was the pirate captain in the story? What happened to him? Where did the men hide?*

Lesson 4

Language	New words and expressions
often, never, sometimes	beer, outdoor, creative, mechanical, indoor,
Simple past	studious, type, fix,
Simple present	all-rounder, life style

Beginning the lesson

- Ask pupils to tell you what they know about pirates. (They attacked treasure ships; They stole gold and jewels; They fought with swords; etc.)
- Ask pupils to tell you things they often do and things they never do: *I often play basketball. I never play tennis*, etc.

PB 27 ex 4 **A pirate's life**

What did pirates often do? What did they never do? Ask a friend.

- Practice asking the questions with the class: *Did pirates steal gold?* (Yes, often.) *Did pirates play tennis?* (No, never.) Pupils continue asking and answering in pairs. Teach the new word *beer*.
- Pupils write down three things pirates often did and three things they never did. Check the answers with the class.

Key

They often attacked ships.
They often carried guns.
They often died young.
They never went to school.
They never rode horses.
They never played tennis.

PB 27 **Imagine you can go back in time.**

Talk to your friend.

- Ask pupils to imagine that they are pirates. Ask them to think about answers to the questions then talk to their partners about their lives as pirates. Pupils can also draw pictures of themselves dressed as pirates.
- Ask pupils to write about a day in their life as a pirate. Ask pupils to write it like a diary. Do a sample day with the whole class: *This morning I got up very early. I had ... for breakfast. We sailed to ...* etc.
- Ask pupils to read about their days to the class.

Read about Susie, Jack and Cathy.

What type of lifestyle do they have?

- Ask pupils to read about Susie, Jack and Cathy. Teach the new words *lifestyle, outdoor, mechanical, creative, type* and *fix*.

- Ask questions: *What does Susie often do?* etc.

- Teach *indoor* and *studious*. Pupils read the questions and check the boxes.

- Pupils ask and answer the questions in pairs. Ask them to decide which type they are. Discuss their answers with the class and teach the word *all-rounder* to describe someone who likes all kinds of activities.

- Pupils can write about themselves and their friends using the same kind of language as the descriptions of Susie, Jack and Cathy.

Ending the lesson

- Pupils tell the class about their partners' lifestyles: *Maria is the studious type. She often ...* etc.

Project ideas

Ships: Pupils can find out more about the kind of ships that pirates sailed in and life at sea.

Lifestyles: Pupils write longer profiles of themselves and their friends, including photos or drawings.

Assessment activity

- Ask pupils to write answers to the following questions:

  1 What did Blackbeard look like?
  2 How did Blackbeard die?
  3 Where did the Spanish treasure ships sail from?
  4 What did pirates often do?
  5 What did pirates never do?

Language review 2

Lesson 1

Language
questions in the past: who, what, when, where, how many, how much

Beginning the lesson

- Ask pupils questions about the recent past: *What did you do yesterday? Where did you go? Who did you meet?* etc.

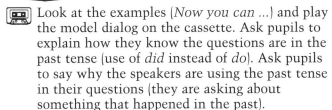 **Asking questions about the past**

Look at the examples (*Now you can ...*) and play the model dialog on the cassette. Ask pupils to explain how they know the questions are in the past tense (use of *did* instead of *do*). Ask pupils to say why the speakers are using the past tense in their questions (they are asking about something that happened in the past).

- Read the questions on the file cards. Ask pupils to think of possible answers to the questions: (I went with my friends etc.)

PB 28 **Things to do**

 1 Play the cassette, pausing for pupils to listen and repeat the questions.

2 Ask pupils to practice making statements about things they did in the past. Their partners ask questions, trying to use as many different question words as possible.

3 Give pupils a time (e.g. last Saturday) or a situation (a vacation) to make up questions about. A real event in the recent past, such as a school trip, would be a useful topic on which to base the questions. Pupils make up their own questions to ask each other.

4 Pupils make cards for their language files.

Ending the lesson

- Ask pupils to imagine situations in which someone would need to ask a lot of questions about the past e.g. an interview on TV or radio, a police investigation, parents asking a child about his/her activities. Pupils can role play one of these situations in pairs or in groups.

Lesson 2

Language	New words and expressions
questions in the past: who, what, when, where, how many, how much	lost and found, membership

Beginning the lesson

- Tell pupils about something you did recently (real or imaginary) e.g. *I went to the zoo.* Ask them to think of as many questions as possible to ask about it.

AB 22 ex A **Write six questions for Rosa.**

- Pupils write the questions, using the question words in the box.
- Check the answers with the class.

  Key

  1 Where in Africa did you go?
  2 Who did you go with?
  3 What did you eat?
  4 How much water did you drink?
  5 How many animals did you see?
  6 When did you come back?

- Ask pupils, working in pairs, to match the questions and the answers. Check the answers with the class.

  Key

  1 Kenya.
  2 Nobody. I traveled alone.
  3 Soup and rice.
  4 Lots – about three liters a day!
  5 Oh, hundreds!
  6 Last Saturday.

- Pupils practice the interview in pairs. Ask them to think of further questions and answers to continue the interview.

- Pupils can write about Rosa using the information from the interview: *Rosa went to Kenya. She traveled ...* etc.

- Pupils interview each other about trips they have taken, and tell the class what they have found out.

Write the questions.

- Look at the form and teach the new words *lost and found* and *membership*. Ask pupils to work out what questions Mike needs to ask to fill in the form. Ask them which questions will be in the past tense.

 Pupils write the questions in their Activity Books. Play the cassette for pupils to check the answers.

Tapescript and key

Mike: Hi! Can I help you?
Boy: Er ... I lost something last week.
Mike: OK. Let's fill in a form. Here we are. First, what is your name?
Boy: Brad Newton.
Mike: B-R-A-D Newton. And what's your membership number, Brad?
Boy: 348.
Mike: OK. And what did you lose?
Boy: I lost a green notebook and a pen.
Mike: What color was the pen?
Boy: Er ... red.
Mike: A red pen. OK. Where did you lose them?
Boy: Er ... outside the office.
Mike: OK. And when did you lose them?
Boy: On Friday.
Mike: What time?
Boy: Er ... about five-thirty.
Mike: Five-thirty. OK Brad, I'll check with the office. Perhaps someone's found your things.

 Play the cassette again, pausing for pupils to fill in the form.

- Ask pupils to make their own forms, like the one in the Activity Book. Pupils interview their partners about things they have lost and fill in the forms.

Ending the lesson

- Pupils tell the class about what their friends have lost. Encourage pupils to ask each other questions: *What did Maria lose? Where did she lose it?* etc.

Lesson 3

Language
Simple past
who, where, what,
what kind of

Beginning the lesson

- Ask questions about pirates: *What did they steal? What did Blackbeard look like? What kind of ships did they have?*

 Skills Review 2: Listening

- Look at the pictures with the class. Ask them to describe the pirates in the pictures.

 Play the first part of the cassette. Pupils listen and point to the pirates.

Tapescript and key

Pegleg was a tall pirate. He always wore gold rings in his ears. Redbelly was short and he wore a red scarf on his head. Greenbeard was a fat pirate. He wore a big black hat. And Scarface was very thin. He had a big black mustache and he wore yellow boots.

 Ask pupils to copy the chart, leaving enough room to write the answers. Then play the second part of the cassette for pupils to write the information about the pirates.

Tapescript

The pirates all had pets. Scarface had a spider. Pegleg had a monkey. It was very naughty. Greenbeard's pet was a parrot. It could talk. And Redbelly had a dog.

Redbelly's ship was called the Black Cat. Pegleg and his men sailed in a ship called the Eagle. The name of Greenbeard's ship was the Mary Jane and the Lion belonged to Scarface.

The pirates all hid their treasure in different places. Redbelly hid his treasure behind a rock on an island. Greenbeard hid his treasure under the ocean. Scarface hid his treasure in a cave and Pegleg hid his treasure on a ship.

- Ask pupils to ask each other questions to check their answers: *What was Pegleg's ship called? What kind of pet did Redbelly have? Where did Greenbeard hide his treasure?* etc.

- Check the answers with the class.

Key

Name	Pegleg	Redbelly	Greenbeard	Scarface
ship	Eagle	Black Cat	Mary Jane	Lion
pet	monkey	dog	parrot	spider
hidden treasure	on a ship	behind a rock on an island	under the ocean	in a cave

29 ## Things to do

1 Pupils practice asking and answering questions about the pirates.
2 Pupils draw pictures of pirates and their ships, then ask and answer questions about them in pairs.

Ending the lesson

• Collect pupils' pirate pictures and distribute them around the class. Ask pupils to find out who drew the pictures by asking questions: *Did your pirate have a red beard?* etc.

Optional lesson 4

Language
Simple past
question words

Beginning the lesson

• Ask pupils to think of question words and make sample questions with them.

More practice with questions about the past

1 Pupils work in groups to write a history quiz with ten questions e.g. *When did ...? Who had a ship called ...?* They can then challenge other groups to answer the questions.
2 Pupils take turns thinking of a historical character. The others must ask questions to find out the identity of the character: *Was this person a man or a woman? Where did s/he live?* etc.
3 Ask pupils to imagine that someone robbed a bank at four o'clock yesterday. Ask the to imagine that they are police officers interviewing people in the area. What questions would they ask? Pupils should write a list of questions then role play the police interviews in groups.

Unit 7   Sam's disappeared!

Background information

Kate and Sam are appearing in a pirate movie which is being shot in Mexico.

Lesson 1

Language	New words and expressions
Present perfect	day off, scriptwriter, reef, explore, octopus, grab, disturb

Beginning the lesson

- Ask questions about the story so far: *Where were Kate and Sam? What did they do in the movie? Who was the star of the movie? What was the movie about?*

PB 30   **Sam's disappeared!**

- Open Pupils' Books at page 30 and discuss the story. Ask pupils to tell you what they think is happening in the story.

- Listen to the cassette. Pupils follow the story in the Pupils' Book.

- Teach the new vocabulary as you ask questions about the story: *day off, scriptwriter, reef, explore, octopus.*

- Play the cassette again, pausing for pupils to repeat.

PB 31 ex 1   **What's happened?**

Listen and match.

- Look at the past participles in the box. Teach *grab* and *disturb.*

- Play the cassette. Pupils listen and find the pictures.

Tapescript and key

Boy: What's happened here?
Girl: Dan's caught a fish.
Boy: It's a big one. (2)
Girl: Yes. And look – here's Sam – he's dived into the sea. He's going swimming. (4)
Boy: What's this?
Girl: It's the reef. Sam's found a hole in the reef. (3) And look! He's seen a box. (5)
Boy: Yes, but he's disturbed an octopus, and it doesn't look very happy! (1)

Girl: It's very angry! Look! It's grabbed Sam's wrist. (6)
Boy: Huuh! What happened?
Girl: Wait and see!

- Play the cassette again, pausing for pupils to listen and repeat.

- Play the model dialog on the cassette for pupils to listen and repeat. Pupils talk about the pictures in pairs.

- Ask questions with the class: *What's happened in picture 1?* (Sam's disturbed an octopus) etc.

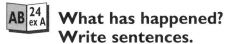   **What has happened? Write sentences.**

- Ask pupils to make up sentences about the pictures in pairs using the past participles in the box.

- Check the answers by asking questions about the pictures: *What's happened in picture 1?* etc.

Key

2 The rabbit has disappeared.
3 The girl's watch has stopped.
4 The thief has broken the window.
5 The spaceship has landed on the moon.
6 The boy has seen a ghost.

Ending the lesson

Game: What's disappeared?

- Divide the class into teams. Send a pupil from each team out of the room. While they are away, remove and hide something from the classroom e.g. a picture from the wall. Invite the pupils back into the classroom. The first one to find out and say what has disappeared: *(The picture) has disappeared!* wins a point for his or her team.

Lesson 2

Language	New words and expressions
Present perfect	bear, tear, spill, knock over, empty, trash can, mess

Beginning the lesson

- Play the game *What's disappeared?* from the previous lesson. Give practice with plurals e.g. *The flowers have disappeared.*

What have they done?

Listen and point.

- Look at the picture with the class and teach the new words: *bear, tear, spill, knock over, empty* and *trash can*.

 Play the cassette, pausing for pupils to find and point to the things in the picture.

Tapescript and key

Bill: Oh no! Look Some bears have been here!
Maggie: They've torn our tent.
Bill: They've broken our plates.
Maggie: They've spilled our milk all over the ground.
Bill: They've climbed onto the table.
Maggie: They've opened our food box.
Bill: Look here! They've eaten all our cookies!
Maggie: They've knocked over the chairs.
Bill: Where's my hat? They've stolen my hat.
Maggie: They've thrown my T-shirt into the river.
Bill: And they've emptied the trash can. What a mess!
Maggie: Have all the bears gone away now?
Bill: I'm not sure.

- Check the answers by asking questions to the whole class: *What have the bears torn?* etc.

 Play the cassette again, pausing for pupils to listen and repeat. Then play the model dialog. Pupils talk about the picture in pairs.

- Ask pupils to find the bears in the picture and say where they have hidden.

Key

One bear has hidden under the table. Another bear has climbed a tree. Another has hidden behind a bush. Another has hidden behind a tree.

 Be a detective. Look at Jack's room and answer the questions.

- Ask pupils to work in pairs to look at the picture and write answers to the questions.
- Check the answers with the whole class.

Key

1 He's eaten a pizza.
2 He's broken a coffee mug.
3 He's opened the window.
4 He's knocked over a chair.
5 He's spilled some coffee.

Ending the lesson

- Do a series of actions e.g. open the door; hide a book and ask pupils to say what you have done: *You've opened ...* etc.

Lesson 3

Language	New words and expressions
Present perfect	goldmine, mining equipment, tool, gold field, block, landslide, sack

Beginning the lesson

- Ask questions in the present perfect: *Has anybody opened the window? Who has opened the window? Have you broken anything this week?* etc.

Goldmine game

Play this game with your friend.

- Read the instructions for the game with the whole class, teaching the new words.
- Pupils play the game in pairs.
- Ask questions about the game: *Where has someone found gold? What did you buy? What did someone steal?* etc.

Write the missing questions.

- Ask pupils to work in pairs to look at the answers and work out the questions, writing them in their Activity Books.
- Check the answers with the whole class.

Key

1 What have you lost?
2 What has she broken?
3 Where have you hidden the box?
4 What have you seen?

- Pupils practice asking and answering the questions in pairs. They can continue the dialogs by asking further questions e.g. *Where did you lose your watch? Can I help you to find it?* etc.

Ending the lesson

- Ask pupils to imagine that they have found a goldmine and work in groups to role play what happens next e.g. they tell their friends about it, they make plans.

Lesson 4

Language	New words and expressions
Present perfect	turn off, heating, electricity port, shipwreck

Beginning the lesson

• Ask pupils to tell you things that they do before they go away on vacation e.g. pack their suitcases, say goodbye to their friends.

 Write the questions.

• Look at the list of things to do with the whole class. Teach the new vocabulary: *turn off, heating* and *electricity.*

• Ask pupils to work in pairs to make questions and write them down in their Activity Books.

Key

Have you packed the suitcase?
Have you put the passports in the bag?
Have you turned off the heating, water and electricity?
Have you closed the windows?
Have you locked the door?

• Pupils can practice asking and answering the questions in pairs.

 Ask pupils to discuss in pairs or groups what other things they have to do before they go away on vacation. They can make lists and practice asking and answering.

 Listen and follow the directions to the shipwreck.

• Look at the map with the whole class. Practice the expressions *to the (west) of* and *to the (east).* Teach the new words *port* and *shipwreck.*

 Play the cassette, pausing for pupils to listen and follow the directions on their maps, drawing the route in pencil.

Tapescript

Sail from the port of Santa Rosa and go north between the islands of Rima and Luna. Rima is the bigger island to your west. Then sail east around the island of Luna. Be careful not to hit the rocks off the north coast. When you see an island with mountains in front of you, turn north and sail up the west coast of this island – it is called Juma. When you reach the north end of Juma you will see a small island with a volcano

to the east. The wreck of the treasure ship is to the west of this island, between the volcano and the island of Pula. Good luck!

• Check the answers with the whole class.

Key

• Talk about the map with the whole class. Ask: *Which island is bigger, Rima or Luna? What is the island with mountains called?* etc.

• Pupils can continue talking about the map in pairs. They could also draw their own treasure maps and talk about them with their partners or groups.

Ending the lesson

Game: Look for gold.

Send two pupils out of the room while the class decide on a place to hide a small object (the gold). When the pupils return, they should ask questions to find the gold: *Is it near the window?* (no) *Is it beside the bookshelves?* (yes) When the answer is *yes,* pupils can move about the classroom.

Project idea

• Looking for gold: Pupils can find out more about the Californian gold rush in the 19th century. They can also find out other places where people have discovered gold.

Assessment activity

• Ask pupils to write answers to the following questions:

1 What have you eaten today?
2 Have you lost anything this week?
3 What games have you played this week?
4 Have you cleaned your room today?
5 Who have you met today?

Unit 8 Under the ocean

Lesson 1

Language	New words and expressions
Present simple *Superlatives* **Adverbs of manner*	cover, surface, creature, coral, tiny, valley, range (of mountains), jellyfish, whale, herring, shark, ray, jaw, breathe, gently, easily, quickly, lazily

* = new language

Beginning the lesson

- Review superlatives. Ask: *Who's the tallest person in the class? Who has the longest hair? What's the heaviest thing in the classroom?* etc. Encourage pupils to ask the same kind of questions.

 Under the ocean

- Open Pupils' Books at page 34 and discuss the pictures on pages 34 and 35 in L1. Ask pupils to tell you what they know about the creatures in the pictures.
- Teach the new words: *coral, valley, jellyfish, whale, herring, shark* and *ray*, referring to the pictures.

 Listen to the cassette. Pupils follow the reading passage in the Pupils' Book.

- Teach the new vocabulary *cover, surface, creature, tiny, range of mountains, jaw, breathe, gently, easily, quickly* and *lazily* as you ask questions.
- Ask pupils to read the passage again in pairs.

 Listen and answer the questions

- Ask pupils to answer yes or no to the questions they hear on the cassette.

 Play the cassette, pausing for pupils to answer the questions.

Tapescript and key

1 Is more than half the earth under the ocean? *(Yes.)*

2 Do many creatures live around coral reefs? *(Yes.)*
3 Are there mountains under the ocean? *(Yes.)*
4 Do jellyfish float near the bottom of the ocean? *(No.)*
5 Do whales and dolphins need to come to the surface of the ocean to breathe? *(Yes.)*
6 Are great white sharks very dangerous? *(Yes.)*
7 Do flat fish live near the surface of the ocean? *(No.)*
8 Is the great white shark the largest creature in the ocean? *(No.)*
9 Do herrings travel together in large numbers? *(Yes.)*
10 Is the Mariana Trench in the Atlantic Ocean? *(No.)*

- Check the answers by asking the questions again with the class.

 Play the cassette again. Pupils listen and repeat the questions.

- Pupils practice asking similar questions in pairs.

AB 27 ex A **What's wrong?**

- Ask pupils to look at the picture in pairs and find out what is wrong, writing their answers in their Activity Books.
- Check the answers with the whole class.

Key

2 Dolphins don't swim at the bottom of the ocean.
3 Rays don't swim near the surface of the ocean.
4 Sharks don't come to the surface to breathe.
5 Octopuses don't have six legs.

- Pupils can talk about the picture in pairs:

A: Do jellyfish swim at the bottom of the ocean?
B: No, they don't. They float near the surface.

Ending the lesson

- Ask pupils to describe and guess sea creatures: *It lives near the bottom of the ocean. It has eight legs*, etc.

Lesson 2

Language	New words and expressions
Past simple *Adverbs of manner* * *How did* *(he swim)?*	strongly, loudly, carefully, knock, tiptoe, doorstep, suddenly, lid, gently secretly, sadly, quietly, quickly

* = new language

Beginning the lesson

- Ask pupils to tell you about creatures that live in the ocean: *Tell me something about octopuses. (They have eight legs.)* etc.

 A play

Listen and read, then read with your friends.

- Look at the picture story with the whole class and teach the new vocabulary: *strongly, loudly, carefully, knock, tiptoe* and *doorstep.*

 Play the cassette. Pupils listen and read.

- Ask questions about the story: *Did the wind blow gently? (No.) How did the wind blow? (It blew strongly.) Who was in the house? (Simon and Alice.) What did Alice say?* etc.

 Play the cassette again, pausing for pupils to listen and repeat.

- Pupils read the story in threes, one pupil telling the story and the others reading the parts of Alice and Simon. They should also make the sound effects (the wind, knocking on the door, etc.).

- Ask some pupils to read the story to the rest of the class. Then tell pupils, in their groups, to think of an ending to the story, and act it out in the same way.

 How do you do these things? Choose one of these words.

- Ask questions about how pupils do different things: *How do you talk when you are in the library? Do you eat your breakfast quickly or slowly? How do you cross the road?*

- Ask pupils to write sentence answers to the questions, then check the answers with the whole class.

Key

1 I hold a baby rabbit *gently.*
2 I write my diary *secretly.*
3 I say goodbye to my best friend *sadly.*

4 I watch birds *quietly.*
5 I swim away from a shark *quickly.*

Ending the lesson

- Pupils can think of more questions with adverbs and ask and answer them with a partner, e.g. *How do you eat an ice cream cone? (Quickly.)* etc.

Lesson 3

Language	New words and expressions
Imperatives	turtle, tunnel, seaweed, anchor
Adverbs of manner	clap your hands, softly, noisily

Beginning the lesson

- Ask pupils to do things: *Maria, please tiptoe to the board quietly. Open the cabinet very slowly and carefully,* etc.

 Under the ocean adventure

Play this game with your friend.

- Look at the game with the class. Teach the new words: *turtle, tunnel, seaweed* and *anchor.*

- Pupils play the game in pairs.

- Ask questions about the game: *Did you get lost? Where?* etc.

 Adverb game

Listen to the cassette and follow the instructions.

- Teach the new vocabulary: *clap your hands, softly* and *noisily.*

 Play the cassette, pausing for pupils to listen and follow the instructions.

Tapescript

Boy: Say hello loudly.
Girl: Say hello softly.
Boy: Now say hello very softly.
Girl: Stand up quickly!
Boy: Now sit down very slowly.
Girl: Pick up your pencil quietly.
Boy: Put your pencil back on your desk very carefully.
Girl: Clap your hands noisily. That's all.

 Play the cassette again. Pupils listen and repeat.

Ending the lesson

- Play *Simon says,* including adverbs in the instructions: *Simon says stand up slowly. Sit down carefully,* etc.

Lesson 4

Language	New words and expressions
Superlatives	aquarium, tentacle

Materials needed

paper, paint, etc. for making posters

Beginning the lesson

- Ask questions with adverbs: *What do you do quietly? What do you do slowly?* etc.

 What color are the fish and rocks in the aquarium? Listen and write the colors.

- Look at the picture and teach the new word *aquarium.*

 Play the cassette, pausing for pupils to write the colors.

Tapescript and key

The biggest fish in the aquarium is blue. I think it's the most beautiful fish.
There's a yellow fish, too. It's the longest fish.
The green fish are smaller than the blue fish, but they're not the smallest fish.
The smallest fish are red.
There are two rocks in the aquarium. One is taller than the other. The taller rock is pink and the shorter, flatter rock is purple.

- Ask questions about the picture: *What color is the biggest fish? Are the red fish smaller than the green ones?* etc.
- Pupils can color the fish. Ask them which fish they think is the most beautiful and which they think is the ugliest.

 Make a poster.

- Put the words and pictures together to make a poster about life in the ocean.
- Read the words for your poster section and teach the new vocabulary.
- Ask pupils to work in pairs to match the words and the pictures.
- Pupils make posters in pairs or groups, copying the pictures and using the words to write captions for their pictures.
- Ask pupils to find out more facts about the ocean to add to their posters.

Ending the lesson

- Play *Simon says.*

Project ideas

- Ocean creatures: Pupils can research different aspects of life under the ocean; e.g. whales and dolphins; life around a coral reef; the fish we eat.
- Under the ocean mobiles: Pupils can cut out and color fish and other sea creatures to make mobiles.

Assessment activity

- Ask pupils to write answers to the following questions:

1 How long can the blue whale stay under the water?
2 How do jellyfish move?
3 What do you know about the great white shark?
4 How do you cross the road?
5 Who is the tallest pupil in your class?

Unit 9 Sam's discovery

Background information

On a day off for the movie crew, Kate and Sam went on a boat with the movie star, Marina, and the scriptwriter, Dan. Sam decided to explore the reef on his own. He found a mysterious box in a hole in the reef, but at the same time he disturbed an octopus.

Lesson 1

Language	New words and expressions
could, couldn't	discovery, rescue, persuade, mysterious,
too, enough	flipper

Beginning the lesson

- Ask questions about the story so far: *Where were Kate and Sam? Where did Sam go? What did he find? What did he disturb? What did the octopus do?*

PB 38 Sam's discovery

- Open Pupils' books at page 38 and talk about the pictures. Ask pupils to tell you what they think is happening in the story.

- 🔲 Listen to the cassette. Pupils follow the story in the Pupils' Book.

- Teach the new vocabulary: *discovery, rescue, persuade* and *mysterious.*

- 🔲 Play the cassette again, pausing for pupils to repeat.

- Pupils read the story again in pairs.

PB 39 ex 1 What could they do?

Listen and answer. Then talk to your friend.

- Ask pupils to look at the story again and answer the questions they hear on the cassette. Teach *flipper.*

- 🔲 Play the cassette, pausing for pupils to listen and answer the questions.

Tapescript and key

Sam: That octopus was very strong. Could I escape on my own? (No, you couldn't.) Could Marina rescue me from the octopus? (Yes, she could.)

Dan picked up one of Kate's flippers by mistake. Could Dan put on Kate's flippers? (No, he couldn't.)
Then we all swam to the reef. Could I find the box again? (Yes, you could.)
We brought the box back to the boat. Could Kate lift it on her own? (Yes, she could.)
Could we open the box? (Yes, you could.)

- 🔲 Play the cassette again, pausing for pupils to repeat Sam's questions.

- Ask questions: *Could Sam escape from the octopus?* (No.) *Why not?* (The octopus was too strong.)

- 🔲 Play the model dialog on the cassette for pupils to listen and repeat.

- Pupils ask and answer questions in pairs.

 Match the sentences about the story in the Pupils' Book.

- Ask pupils to draw lines to make true sentences about the story. Check the answers with the class.

Key

2 Marina could rescue Sam.
3 They could open the box.
4 Kate could lift the box.
5 They couldn't find any treasure in the box.

Ending the lesson

- Ask pupils to try to do things in the classroom (some possible, others not) then ask questions with could: *Could Maria touch the top of the window? Could Carlos lift the table?* etc.

Lesson 2

Language	New words and expressions
could, couldn't	narrow, wide, shallow, crowded,
too, enough	comfortable

Beginning the lesson

- Ask questions and encourage pupils to make answers with *too* and *enough: Can you touch the ceiling?* (No, it's too high. No, I'm not tall enough.) etc.

Find a new home for the octopus.

Read and find the best place for the octopus to live.

- Read the adjectives in the box and teach the new words.

 Play the model dialog on the cassette for pupils to listen and repeat.

- Ask pupils to look at the picture in pairs and decide which place would be the best one for the octopus's new home.

- Check the answers with the class by asking questions: *How about A? No, it's too dangerous,* etc.

Key

A is too dangerous.
B is too light. It isn't dark enough.
C is too narrow. It isn't wide enough.
D is too big. It isn't small enough.
E is too crowded.
F is the best place for the octopus to live.

- Pupils can write sentences about the possible homes for the octopus.

 Complete Sharon's description of a day at the beach.

- Ask pupils to complete the sentences, using the expressions in the box.

- Check the answers with the whole class.

Key

We couldn't swim underwater. It was too shallow.
We couldn't make coffee. The water was not hot enough.
We couldn't eat our sandwiches. They were too dirty.
We couldn't buy burgers. They were too expensive.

- Pupils can ask and answer questions in pairs:

A: Why couldn't they move the boat?
B: It was too heavy.

Ending the lesson

- Ask pupils to tell you about trips they have made themselves when things went wrong. (We couldn't have a picnic because it rained etc.).

Lesson 3

Language	New words and expressions
Simple past	sailing ship, piece, china, owner, cargo, dish, wooden,
would like to	as good as new, sink, gold bar

Beginning the lesson

- Ask about the story: *What did Sam think was in the box? What was really in the box? Why do people look for treasure?* Tell pupils that they are going to read about some real treasure from the ocean.

 Treasure from the ocean

Read about the treasure ship.

- Look at the pictures and teach the new vocabulary: *sailing ship, piece, china, owner, cargo, dish, wooden, as good as new, sink* and *gold bar.*

 Listen to the cassette. Pupils follow the passage in the Pupils' Book.

- Write questions on the board: *What was the name of the treasure ship? Which port did it leave? Where did it sink? How many people escaped from the wreck? Where did they find the dishes? What else did they find?*

- Ask pupils to read the passage and find the answers to the questions in pairs.

Key

The Geldermalsen; Whampoa, in China; in the South China Sea; forty-four; in the 1980s; in wooden chests; packed in tea; gold bars.

 Play the model dialog on the cassette. Pupils listen and repeat.

- In pairs or groups, pupils role play interviews between reporters and divers.

- Ask pupils to repeat their interviews for the rest of the class.

 A treasure chest?

What would you like to do with the treasure?

 Play the model dialog on the cassette for pupils to listen and repeat.

- Pupils talk about what they would like to do with the treasure in pairs or groups.

Treasure hunters' game

- Explain the game. Pupils must follow the arrows to find the shipwreck, choosing the best way to go.
- Pupils play the game in pairs. Encourage them to talk about the game in English: *Which way shall we go? Let's go this way*, etc.

Ending the lesson

- Ask pupils to tell the rest of the class what they would like to do if they found some treasure.

Lesson 4

Language	New words and expressions
could, couldn't	parking lot, meadow, pool, trail

Beginning the lesson

- Practice *left* and *right*. Give pupils instructions: *Raise your right hand. Touch your left ear. Turn right*, etc.

 Joe's family went for a picnic in the mountains. Look at the map and listen.

- Look at the map with the class and teach the new words: *parking lot, meadow, pool* and *trail*.

 Play the cassette. Pupils listen and draw a line on the map to show which way Joe and his family went.

Tapescript

Girl: Which way did you go, Joe? Did you turn left or right at the parking lot?

Joe: We turned left. We couldn't turn right because the bridge was broken.

Girl: Oh. Did you go to Katie's Meadow?

Joe: No. We couldn't cross the river. It was too deep. So we turned left and went to Deer Pool.

Girl: Did you have your picnic at Deer Pool?

Joe: No, we couldn't. It was too wet around Deer Pool for a picnic. So we continued along the trail.

Girl: Did you go along the old forest trail?

Joe: No, we couldn't go along the old forest trail. It was closed. It was too dangerous.

Girl: Did you go to the old gold mine?

Joe: Yes. It was interesting.

Girl: Did you have your picnic there?

Joe: No. We went to Green Hill and we had our picnic there.

- Check the answers with the class.

 Play the cassette again. Pupils listen and mark the places where Joe and his family couldn't go.

Key

- Ask pupils to write sentences about the places they couldn't go, and check their answers in pairs.
- Check the answers with the class.

Key

2 They couldn't go to Katie's Meadow.
3 They couldn't have their picnic at Deer Pool.
4 They couldn't go along the old forest trail.

- Ask questions: *Why couldn't they cross the bridge? (Because it was broken.)* etc.
- Pupils can continue asking and answering questions about the map in pairs.

Opposites crossword

- Find the opposites of these words to complete the crossword puzzle.
- Ask pupils to work in pairs to complete the crossword puzzle.
- Check the answers with the class.

Key

Down: dangerous **1** cold **2** dark **3** long **4** big **5** early **6** narrow **7** good **8** quick **9** sad

Ending the lesson

Game: Opposites game

Divide the class into three or four teams. Invite the first player in each team to the board. Say an adjective e.g. *long*. The first player to write the opposite of long on the board wins a point for his or her team.

Project idea

- Pupils could find out about and write and draw maps, plans and pictures of real life treasure, perhaps something that archaeologists have found in their own country.

Assessment activity

- Ask pupils to write questions for the following answers:

  1 No, we couldn't. It was too expensive.
  2 No, he couldn't. The octopus was too strong.
  3 No, I couldn't. I wasn't old enough.
  4 Yes, I could.
  5 Yes, they could.

Language review 3

Lesson 1

Language
Comparatives
Superlatives

Beginning the lesson

- Ask questions with comparatives and superlatives about people and things in the classroom: *Are you taller than Maria? Who's the tallest person in the class?* etc.

PB 42 Comparatives and superlatives

- Look at the examples of comparatives and superlatives in the file card and play the model dialog on the cassette. Ask pupils to explain what the sentences mean in L1. Ask them also to explain in L1 how the comparatives and superlatives are formed (by adding -er and -est to short adjectives and by adding *more* and *the most* to long ones).

- Ask pupils to think of sample sentences using the comparatives and superlatives in the second file card: *An elephant is stronger than a horse*, etc.

AB 33 ex A Complete the table with comparatives and superlatives.

- Ask pupils to complete the table, working in pairs. Check the answers with the whole class.

  Key

ADJECTIVE	COMPARATIVE	SUPERLATIVE
easy	easier	the easiest
fierce	fiercer	the fiercest
neat	neater	the neatest
good	better	the best
beautiful	more beautiful	the most beautiful
dark	darker	the darkest
slow	slower	the slowest
sad	sadder	the saddest

AB 33 ex B Write comparative sentences about these two pirates.

- Ask pupils to look at the pictures of the pirates and write sentences about them.

- Check the answers with the class. Ask questions: *Who is richer, Tom or Fred?* etc.

Key

2 Terrible Tom is richer than Fearless Fred.
3 Terrible Tom's beard is longer than Fearless Fred's.
4 Fearless Fred's ship is bigger than Terrible Tom's.
5 Fearless Fred's crew is fiercer than Terrible Tom's.
6 Terrible Tom's hat is wider than Fearless Fred's.

- Pupils can continue to talk about the pirates in pairs: *Is Terrible Tom's beard shorter than Fred's? Does Fred have a smaller ship than Tom?* etc.

Ending the lesson

Play a guessing game. One player thinks of an animal, and asks pupils to ask questions with comparatives to find out what the animal is. The player thinking of the animal can answer *yes* or *no*: *Is it bigger than a dog? Does it have a shorter tail than a cat?* etc.

Lesson 2

Language	New words and expressions
Comparatives	taste, flavor
Superlatives	

Beginning the lesson

- Ask pupils to ask each other questions using comparatives and superlatives.

PB 42 Things to do

1 Ask pupils to think of adjectives. A good way to start is to think of an adjective, then think of its opposite: big/small, wide/narrow, etc. Pupils can work in pairs or groups to list as many adjectives as possible, with their comparatives and superlatives.

- Check pupils' answers with the whole class.

2 In pairs or groups, pupils ask questions using the adjectives they have listed.

3 Pupils make file cards, drawing pictures and writing sentences e.g. tall – taller – the tallest (trees, buildings); long – longer – the longest (snakes).

At the Fair. Look at the pictures and write sentences with superlatives.

- Look at the pictures with the class and read the example. Ask pupils to write sentences about the pictures.

- Check the answers with the class.

Key

2 Kevin's horse was the fastest.
3 Jenny's dog was the most beautiful.
4 Jack's watermelon was the biggest.

- Ask questions: *Whose watermelon was the biggest?* etc.

 Which ice cream flavor was the most popular? Listen and complete the chart.

- Look at the chart. Explain that five points are given to the flavor that the person liked best, four points to the next, etc. (Therefore Peter's favorite flavor was strawberry.)

 Play the cassette. Pupils listen and complete the chart.

Tapescript

Woman: What did you think of the ice cream flavors, Peter?
Peter: I thought the strawberry flavor was the best. Then I liked coffee, and next ... um ... chocolate. I didn't like the banana or the orange, but I thought the banana was better than the orange. The orange flavor was the worst.
Woman: How about you, Tina?
Tina: I thought the coffee ice cream was the best. Then the chocolate, next the banana, then the orange. I thought the strawberry was the worst.
Woman: What did you think, Sharon?
Sharon: The chocolate one was the best. It had the most interesting flavor. After that I liked the banana, then the coffee, then the orange. I didn't like the strawberry one much.
Woman: What did you think, Jack?
Jack: I thought the banana was the best flavor. Then the chocolate, then the strawberry. Then ... um ... the coffee, and last the orange.

- Check the answers with the class. Ask questions (*Which flavor did Tina say was the best?* etc.) and write the answers on the board.

Key

	Peter	Tina	Sharon	Jack
Strawberry	5	1	1	3
Chocolate	3	4	5	4
Coffee	4	5	3	2
Banana	2	3	4	5
Orange	1	2	2	1

- Ask pupils to add up the marks and find out which flavor was the most popular.

Key

The chocolate ice cream was the most popular.

- Ask pupils, working in groups, to make their own charts to do a survey of e.g. different kinds of soft drinks or snacks.

Ending the lesson

- Ask pupils to devise a competition in the classroom e.g. to find out who has the neatest desk; the cleanest shoes; the most beautiful handwriting.

Lesson 3

Language	New words and expressions
Comparatives	seaweed, eel

Beginning the lesson

- Ask pupils to look carefully at and compare things that are almost the same; e.g. two flowers or two apples. Ask them to find as many differences as they can between the two: *This flower is darker; this apple is heavier;* etc.

PB 43 | **Speaking**

- Look at the words in the boxes and teach the new vocabulary.

- Ask pupils to work in pairs to find the differences between the two pictures.

- Check the answers with the class. Ask pupils to tell you what is different.

Key

The jellyfish is smaller in picture 2.
The diver is deeper in picture 2.
The eel is longer in picture 2.
The shark is more dangerous in picture 2.
The shark's teeth are sharper in picture 2.
The fish are more colorful in picture 2.
The octopus is lighter in picture 2.

The treasure chest is bigger in picture 2.
The seaweed is shorter in picture 2.
The rock is smaller in picture 2.

PB 43 Things to do

1 Ask pupils, working in pairs, to ask and answer questions about the pictures, following the example.

2 Ask pupils to write sentences about the pictures, using the words in the box. Check their answers with the key.

Ending the lesson

• Ask pupils each to draw a picture of, for example, an octopus or a treasure chest, then in pairs or groups to compare their pictures: *Whose octopus is the fiercest? biggest? friendliest? Whose treasure chest is the strongest? smallest? most interesting?* etc.

Optional Lesson 4

Beginning the lesson

• Ask pupils, working in groups, to write down as many adjectives with their comparative and superlative forms as they can think of within a time limit.

More practice with comparatives and superlatives

1 Ask pupils to talk or write about other things they are studying e.g. geography (Australia is bigger than New Zealand) or science. They can use reference material to make sure their data is accurate.

2 Pupils can work in teams to make up quizzes involving comparative and superlative questions: *Is Tokyo bigger than Washington? What's the highest mountain in the world?*

3 Consumer survey: Do a more elaborate version of the activity in exercise D in the Activity Book. Bring to class a selection of drinks or food for pupils to taste and compare e.g. different brands of orange drinks or potato chips. Pupils can compare not only the taste (A is sweeter than B; X is saltier than Y) but also the prices and the designs of the packaging.

Ending the lesson

• Pupils report on the results of their consumer survey, explaining the charts they have made, etc.

Unit 10   Mysteries of the ocean

Background information

Nobody knows the location of Atlantis, if it ever existed, but the Azores, where the Marie Celeste was found, and the Sargasso Sea can be found on a map.

Lesson 1

Language	New words and expressions
Simple past	mystery, three-quarters, cover, tiny,
Simple present	solve, puzzle, normal, storm, writer, golden, force, destroy, fact, opinion, maybe

Beginning the lesson

- Discuss mysteries in L1. Ask pupils if they enjoy reading about mysterious happenings. Why do they think real life mysteries interest people?

 Mysteries of the ocean

- Open Pupils' Books at page 44 and talk about the pictures in L1. Ask pupils to tell you anything they already know about the Marie Celeste, Atlantis and the Bermuda Triangle.

 Listen to the cassette. Pupils follow the text in the Pupils' Book.

- Ask questions, teaching the new vocabulary for each section of the text.

PB 45 ex 1 **Fact or opinion?**

- Teach the new words: *fact* and *opinion*. Ask pupils to give examples of facts e.g. *There are some flowers on the table. The sun is shining.* Then ask them to give examples of opinions e.g. *The flowers are beautiful. The weather is too hot.*

- Ask pupils to read the sentences in pairs and say whether they express facts or opinions.

Key

Many ships have disappeared in the Sargasso Sea is a fact. The other sentences are opinions.

- Ask pupils to read the passages again in pairs and find the examples of facts and opinions.

- Check the answers with the whole class, discussing why they think the sentences are facts or opinions.

Key

Opinions about Atlantis: The people who lived there were smart scientists and engineers. Some scientists think that the ruins of Atlantis are under the ocean. Others think a huge volcano destroyed the city.

Fact about Atlantis: The Greek writer, Plato, wrote about a beautiful city on an island in the Atlantic Ocean.

Facts about the Marie Celeste: The Marie Celeste left New York in October 1872. On December 3rd a ship found the Marie Celeste in the middle of the Atlantic Ocean off the Azores. The captain's log book finished on November 25th but it did not say what happened.

Opinion about the Marie Celeste: Maybe the crew died in a storm.

Facts about the Bermuda Triangle: In 1945 five airplanes flew over this part of the ocean. Suddenly they sent a radio message. Then they all disappeared.

Opinion about the Bermuda Triangle: Maybe there is a strong force which destroys the ships and airplanes.

Ending the lesson

- Ask pupils to give their opinions and say what they think happened to the Marie Celeste. Help them to make sentences beginning *I think ...* or *Maybe ...*

Lesson 2

Language	New words and expressions
Simple past	spin, engine

Beginning the lesson

- Ask questions about the reading passages on pages 44 and 45 of the Pupils' Book: *What happened to the Marie Celeste? Where did they find the ship? What did they find on the ship? What do you think happened to the crew?*

Captain Don Henry took his ship the _Good News_ through the Bermuda Triangle in 1966. Listen to his story, then choose the right words.

• Read the questions with the class. Teach the new words _spin_ and _engine_.

 Play the cassette. Pupils listen and circle the correct answers. Play the cassette again for pupils to check their answers.

Tapescript

In 1966 I was captain of the _Good News_. We went through the Sargasso Sea. The weather was very good. There was no wind. Suddenly, something very strange happened. The ship's compass started to go around very fast. I looked out at the ocean. I could only see a big white cloud. I couldn't see the ocean or sky. Then the ship's engine stopped. The lights went out. The white cloud covered the ship. The ship started to move up and down. A strong force started to pull the ship backwards into the white cloud. We were all very frightened. I tried to start the engine again. At last it started and we started to move very slowly forward. Something tried to pull us back into the cloud, but we escaped. We were very lucky.

Key

1 The weather was very good.
2 The ship's compass started to spin fast.
3 The captain could see a white cloud.
4 The ship's engine stopped.
5 A force tried to pull the ship into the cloud.
6 The _Good News_ escaped.

 Play the cassette again and then ask questions about the listening passage: _What was the ship's name? What was the weather like? Was it windy?_

• Ask pupils to work in pairs or groups to think of an explanation of what happened. Ask pupils to tell the class what they think.

 Find the missing words for this table in your Pupils' Book.

• Ask pupils to work in pairs to find the missing words and complete the table.

• Check the answers with the whole class.

Key

mystery/mysterious; danger/dangerous; storm/stormy; beauty/beautiful; gold/golden

• Ask pupils to work out in pairs what the adjectives could be used to describe.

• Check the answers with the class.

Key

The Bermuda Triangle: mysterious, dangerous
Atlantis: mysterious, beautiful, golden
The Marie Celeste: mysterious

 Read about the mysteries of the ocean in the Pupils' Book. Can you find the words?

• Ask pupils to work in pairs to read the passages again and find the words.

• Check the answers with the whole class.

Key

1 a mystery 2 breakfast 3 the crew 4 storm
5 log book 6 triangle 7 Greek

1 New York 2 the Azores 3 the Sargasso Sea
4 the North Atlantic Ocean 5 Plato

Ending the lesson

• Ask pupils, working in pairs or groups, to act out an interview with Captain Don Henry, asking him questions about his experiences in the Bermuda Triangle.

Lesson 3

Language	New words and expressions
Simple past _Present perfect_	rescue service, lifeboat

Beginning the lesson

• Ask questions about the ocean: _Is it dangerous? What happens when the weather is bad? Have you ever seen a storm at sea?_ etc.

 Rescue at sea

• Put the sentences in the correct order to tell the story.

• Teach the new words: _rescue service_ and _lifeboat_.

• Ask pupils to work in pairs to put the sentences in the correct order to tell the story.

 Play the cassette. Pupils listen and check their answers.

Tapescript and key

Richard and Tanya were on vacation by the ocean.
They had a rubber boat.
Richard wanted to sail the boat over to a small island.
Tanya didn't want to go because it was too dangerous.
Richard sailed off in the boat.
The wind started to blow.
The wind blew the boat out to sea.
Tanya ran to a telephone.
She called the rescue service.
The lifeboat crew rescued Richard.

- Pupils ask and answer questions about the story in pairs.
- Pupils work in pairs to write the conversation between Richard and Tanya then act it out.
- Ask pairs of pupils to act out their conversations for the rest of the class.

 Ask and answer.

 Play the model dialog on the cassette. Pupils listen and repeat.

- Pupils ask and answer the other questions in pairs or groups.
- Ask the questions with the whole class. Ask pupils to tell you more details about their experiences (When did this happen? What happened next? Who was with you? etc).
- Read the story in exercise 2 again. Ask pupils to write about their own experiences in the same way; start by saying where they were, and then write about the things that happened.

 Don has lost a lot of things this year. Write five questions starting When? What? and Where?

- Ask pupils to write the questions about Don in their Activity Books.
- Check the answers with the class.
- Pupils ask and answer the questions in pairs: *What did he lose at the park?* (His baseball cap) etc.

Ending the lesson

- Ask pupils to read their stories from exercise 3 to the rest of the class.

Lesson 4

Language	New words and expressions
Present perfect	life jacket, compass, rescue flare

Materials needed
Dice or spinners for the game

Beginning the lesson

- Ask pupils to imagine that they are planning a trip by boat to an island in the sea. What do they need to take with them?

 Lost at sea

Play this game with your friend.

- Read the instructions with the class and ask pupils to make markers (one each) for the game. Teach the new words: *life jacket, compass* and *rescue flare.*
- Pupils play the game in pairs.

 Fact or opinion? Write Fact (F) or Opinion (O) beside these statements.

- Ask pupils to read the instructions in pairs and write F (fact) or O (opinion) in the boxes.
- Check the answers with the whole class.

Key

1 Brenda made these cookies. (F)
2 They taste horrible! (O)
3 She made them with coconut. (F)
4 I think they taste like dog biscuits. (O)
5 I think she put too much salt in them. (O)
6 She made them for the party, but nobody ate them. (F)

AB 37 ex F **What do you think these ink blots look like?**

- Explain to pupils that they should give their own opinions about what the ink blots look like.
- Pupils discuss what they think the blots look like in pairs, then write their answers in their Activity Books: *I think it looks like ...* etc.
- Discuss pupils' answers with the whole class.

Ending the lesson

- Ask pupils to give facts and opinions about different subjects, e.g. a movie or a TV program they have seen recently, a place or a famous person.

Project idea

• Sea mysteries: Pupils can find out more about the sea mysteries in the Pupils' Book, and about other strange things that have happened at sea.

Assessment activity

• Ask pupils to write questions for the following answers.

1 It left New York in October 1872.
2 I lost it in the park.
3 Yes, I have. I was lost in the forest.
4 The weather was stormy.
5 No, I haven't brought a drink.

Unit 11 Jake Jones's diary

Background information

While exploring the reef, Sam found a mysterious box. Sam hoped the box contained Jake Jones's treasure, but it was too light. At first they thought that the box was empty, but then Dan saw something interesting ...

Lesson 1

Language	New words and expressions
Present perfect	amazing, desert, weak, river bed
Simple present	

Beginning the lesson

- Ask questions about the story: *Who found the box? What did Sam think was in the box? Was the box full of treasure? What was in it?*

PB 48 Jake Jones's diary

- Open the Pupils' Books at page 48 and talk about the pictures. Ask pupils to tell you what they think is happening in the story.

 Listen to the cassette. Pupils follow the story in the Pupils' Book.

- Ask questions about the pictures, teaching the new vocabulary for each picture.

 Play the cassette again, pausing for pupils to repeat.

- In pairs, pupils ask questions about the story.

PB 49 ex 1 Which way did Jake Jones go?

Listen and find the places on the map.

- Look at the map with the class. Teach *river bed*.

 Play the cassette, pausing for pupils to listen and point to the places on the map.

Tapescript and key

Sam: I don't understand Jake's map.
Dan: Well, let's have a look. Can you see the mountains in the northwest?
Marina: Yes, here they are.
Dan: Well, General Delgado's silver mines were in those mountains. Jake stole the treasure at a place called Cortes near the mines. There were six horses carrying gold coins and other things to General Delgado.
Kate: I've found it! What did Jake do then?
Dan: Jake wanted to get back to his ship. It was on the coast, near where we are now. He went south to the Rio Diablo.
Sam: Here! Is that where he camped?
Dan: Yes. He camped somewhere around here on the night of June 15th. He wrote that in his diary.
Marina: But he didn't follow the river to the coast.
Dan: No, he went across the Santa Rosa desert.
Kate: Why did he do that?
Dan: I'm not sure. But I think he couldn't follow the river because there were soldiers at San Antonio.
Kate: Here it is! San Antonio!
Sam: So he decided to cross the desert.
Dan: Yes, but it was very difficult. Jake didn't have enough food and water for his men and horses. And General Delgado and his soldiers were following him.
Sam: What did he do?
Dan: I think Jake decided to bury the treasure in the desert, near Santa Rosa. He could move faster without the treasure.
Marina: And he planned to go back for the treasure later.
Dan: Yes. He crossed the mountains near the coast and found his ship.
Kate: I can see the mountains on the map.
Dan: General Delgado was close behind him.
Sam: And they had a great battle, and the general won.
Kate: But did Jake go back to Santa Rosa for the treasure?
Dan: Mm ... I don't think he did. Jake Jones died in Jamaica two years later. He was a poor man then.
Marina: You mean the treasure's still there!
Dan: Well, yes. I think it is.
Kate: At Santa Rosa? Near Rick Morell's house?
Sam: What are we waiting for? Let's go there!

- Ask questions about the story: *Where did Jake steal the treasure? Where did he go first? Where did he camp for the first night?* etc.

A diary of a trip. Read and match.

- Pupils read the sentences and match them with the pictures.
- Check the answers with the class.

  Key

  Day 1: C Day 2: E Day 3: B Day 4: A Day 5: D

- Ask questions about the diary: *What happened on Day 1? Where were they on Day 4? When did they reach the river?* etc.

 Write sentences with *could* and *couldn't* about the trip in Exercise A.

- Ask pupils to write sentences about the trip in Exercise A.
- Check the answers with the class.

  Key

  Day 2: They couldn't cross the river.
  Day 3: They couldn't find any water.
  Day 4: Their horses could drink.
  Day 5: They could see their ship.

Ending the lesson

Help pupils to retell the story of Jake Jones and his treasure, starting from when he stole the treasure.

Lesson 2

Language	New words and expressions
Simple past	rollerskating, art gallery, dentist
time expressions with ago	

Beginning the lesson

- Teach *ago*. Ask questions: *What day was it two days ago? What time was it an hour ago? Where were you three hours ago?*

 Maria's diary

Look at the things Maria has done this week. Then listen and answer the questions.

- Look at the diary with the class. Teach the new vocabulary *rollerskating, art gallery* and *dentist*. Ask pupils to match the diary entries with the pictures. Ask questions: *What did Maria do on Wednesday? What happened on Monday?* etc.

 Play the cassette, pausing for pupils to answer the questions.

Tapescript and key

It's Saturday now.
What was Maria doing yesterday?
(She went to the dentist in the morning.
She went to school in the afternoon.)
What did she do after school two days ago?
(She went rollerskating.)
Where did she go three days ago?
(She went to an art gallery.)
What kind of test did she have four days ago?
(She had a history test.)
What did she do at school five days ago?
(She practiced her song for the school concert.)
Did she go anywhere six days ago?
(No, she didn't.)

 Play the model dialog on the cassette. Pupils listen and repeat.

- Pupils continue talking about Maria's week in pairs.

Ending the lesson

- Ask questions about pupils' lives with *ago: Did you live here three years ago? Could you ride a bike two years ago?* etc. Encourage pupils to ask each other the same questions.

Lesson 3

Language	New words and expressions
Simple past	the past week
ago	

Beginning the lesson

- Ask questions about things pupils have done in the past week: *What sports have you played? What did you do on Saturday?* etc.

 My diary

Write your own diary for the past week. Then talk to your friend.

- Ask pupils to write their own diaries, like the one in Exercise 2 in the Pupils' Book.

 Play the model dialog on the cassette. Pupils listen and repeat.

- Pupils talk about their diaries in pairs.
- Ask questions with the whole class: *Were you at school two days ago? Where were you? What did you do?*

Paul is a detective. Listen to Paul's report and write the times and dates.

- Look at the pictures with the class. Ask pupils to say what they think is happening in the pictures.

 Play the cassette, pausing for pupils to listen and write the dates and times in the pictures in their Activity Books.

Tapescript

Paul:	So I followed "Fingers" Brown to New York.
Woman:	When did you follow her to New York?
Paul:	A month ago.
Woman:	Let's see. It's June 20th.
Paul:	That's right. I was in New York on May 20th.
Woman:	Hmm.
Paul:	I took this photo of her there.
Woman:	I see. When did you take the photo?
Paul:	Ten days ago.
Woman:	Mmm ...
Paul:	Then she bought a ticket to Los Angeles.
Woman:	And when was that?
Paul:	Two days ago.
Woman:	And when did she catch the airplane?
Paul:	Just six hours ago.
Woman:	Did you see her at the airport?
Paul:	Yes. She met a man in black two hours ago.
Woman:	Well, where are they now?
Paul:	I don't know. They disappeared ten minutes ago.
Woman:	Oh, no!

- Check the answers with the whole class. Ask questions: *When did Paul follow Fingers to New York?* etc.

Key

1 May 20th **2** June 10th **3** June 18th
4 10:00 **5** 11:50

- Pupils can continue talking about the pictures in pairs. They can also write Paul's notes (On May 20th I followed "Fingers" Brown to New York. On ...) etc.

 Tell the truth. Answer the questions about yourself using "ago".

- Ask pupils to write answers to the questions, then talk about their answers in pairs or groups.

- Check pupils' answers with the whole class.

Ending the lesson

Game: Dates and times

Divide the class into teams. Ask questions involving dates and times, e.g. *What day was it eight days ago? What was the date 150 years ago? What time was it 15 minutes ago?* The first team to answer the question correctly wins a point.

Lesson 4

Language	New words and expressions
Present simple like, hate + ing	relax, spend time

Beginning the lesson

- Ask pupils about things they like doing: *Do you like listening to music? Do you like walking in the country?* and things they hate doing: *Do you hate cleaning your room?* etc. Encourage pupils to ask the same kind of questions.

 All about Rick Morell

Imagine your are Rick. Listen and answer the questions.

- Ask pupils to read the magazine article about Rick Morell. Teach the new vocabulary *relax* and *spend time.*

- Ask pupils to say what kind of things Rick Morell likes doing: (He likes painting. He doesn't like going to parties. He likes eating, etc.)

 Play the cassette, pausing for pupils to answer the questions, playing the part of Rick.

Tapescript and key

Reporter:	I'm here at the home of Rick Morell in Mexico City. Rick is relaxing beside his swimming pool. Hello, Rick.
Rick:	Hi! Meet my friends.
Reporter:	Do you like spending time with your friends, Rick?
Rick:	(Yes, I do.). Do you like parties? (No, I hate parties.) You have another house in the desert. What do you like doing there? (I like painting.). Do you like eating, Rick? (Yes, I do.). How about cooking? (I hate cooking.). I believe you write songs, too, Rick. Do you enjoy writing them? (Yes, I do.).

Play the cassette again. Pupils listen and repeat the questions.

- Pupils role play the interview with Rick Morell in pairs.

 ## There's a time to laugh

Song.

- Teach the song in the usual way.

 ## Interview your friend.

- Discuss the kind of questions pupils might like to ask with the whole class. Pupils should try to think of questions which will elicit interesting answers e.g. *What do you like doing when you go out with your friends? What's your favorite TV program and why? Who would you like to meet?*

- Pupils write their questions in their Activity Books then ask their partners the questions and write down their replies.

- Check the answers with the whole class.

- Ask pupils to look again at the magazine article about Rick on page 51 of the Pupils' Book, then write similar articles about their friends in their Activity Books.

- Ask pupils to read out their articles to the rest of the class.

Ending the lesson

Sing the song: *There's a time to laugh.*

Project idea

- Keeping diaries: Pupils write their own diaries in English each week and compare notes at the end of the week.

Assessment activity

- Ask pupils to write answers to the following questions:

1 Where were you three days ago?
2 Could you speak English four years ago?
3 Do you like playing computer games?
4 What do you like doing after school?
5 Is there anything you hate doing? What is it?

Unit 12   What kind of music do you like?

Lesson 1

Language	New words and expressions
What kind of ...?	rock music, reggae, rap,
can/can't	country music, good at,
would like to ...	saxophone, trumpet, flute

Beginning the lesson

- Discuss pupil's favorite kinds of music and performers in L1. Ask if they can play any musical instruments.

PB 52/53 **What kind of music do you like?**

Listen to an interview with Josh and Clare and answer the questions.

- Look at the questions about Josh and Clare with the whole class.
- Teach the new vocabulary: *rock music, reggae, rap, country music, good at* and *band.*

 Then play the cassette, pausing for pupils to answer the questions.

Tapescript and key

Interviewer:	Hello, what are your names?
Clare:	Clare.
Josh:	Josh.
Interviewer:	What kind of music do you both like?
Clare:	I like reggae music and rap, but Josh doesn't like it very much.
Josh:	No. My favorite music is rock music. That's great. I don't like country music.
Interviewer:	Can you play an instrument?
Josh:	I can play the guitar.
Interviewer:	Are you good at playing the guitar?
Josh:	Very good.
Interviewer:	What about you, Clare?
Clare:	I can play the piano. And I'm learning to play the drums.
Interviewer:	And what do you want to do when you're older?
Clare:	We want to be in a band. We want to travel around and make lots of records.
Josh:	Yeah. We want to be famous pop stars and make a number one record.
Interviewer:	Well, I hope you do! Thank you very much.

- Ask questions about the interview with the whole class. *What kind of music does Clare like? (Reggae music and rap.)* etc.

PB 52 ex 1 **What kind of music do you like?**

Make a list with your friend.

- Ask pupils to work in pairs to make lists of the kinds of music they like.
- Then ask pupils to tell the rest of the class what they and their partners like. *My favorite kind of music is (rock) but (Maria) likes (country)* etc.

PB 52 ex 2 **Musical instruments**

Read and match.

- Ask pupils to match the musical instruments with the pictures.
- Check the answers by asking pupils to point to the instruments in the pictures. Ask questions about the instruments: *Can you play the piano? Are you good at playing the piano? Which instrument would you like to play? What's your favorite musical instrument? Can you play it?* etc.

PB 52 ex 3 **An interview**

Listen to the interview with Josh and Clare again and repeat the questions.

 Play the interview with Josh and Clare again, pausing for pupils to repeat the questions.

- Ask pupils to interview each other, asking the same questions.

AB 41 ex A **Can you read music?**

- Ask pupils to read the music and match the letters with the pictures.

Key

2 bag **3** bed **4** badge **5** bee

Ending the lesson

- Ask pupils to tell the class about their partners' answers to the questions in exercise 3. (*Maria likes pop music. She can't play a musical instrument but she'd like to play the guitar.*)

Preparation for Lesson 2

- Ask pupils to bring to class pictures and records or cassettes of their favorite music.

Lesson 2

Language	New words and expressions
Present simple	go on tour, equipment,
Present passive	sound engineer,
would like	lighting engineer, roadie,
	recording studio, record live,
	producer, album,
	video director, storyboard,
	mime
Materials needed	
pupils' pictures and records or cassettes	

Beginning the lesson

- Ask pupils to tell their friends about their favorite music. Ask them to prepare something to tell the class about their favorite bands or singers.

 Would you like to be a pop star?

Read and find out.

- Discuss the pictures on page 53 in L1. Ask pupils to tell you what the people in the pictures are doing.

 Listen to the cassette. Pupils follow the reading passage in the Pupils' Book.

- Teach the new vocabulary: *go on tour, equipment, sound engineer, lighting engineer, roadie, recording studio, record live, producer, album, video director, story board* (look at the example on page 55), *film* and *mime* as you ask questions about the reading passage: *What does a band need when it goes on tour? Who are the people who go with the band? What do the sound engineers do? Who looks after the lighting?* etc.

 What would you like to be?

Talk to your friend.

 Play the model dialog on the cassette for pupils to listen and repeat.

 Pupils talk about what they would like to be in pairs.

- Ask questions with the whole class: *What would you like to be? Who would like to be a lighting engineer? Would you like to be a video director?* etc.

- Ask pupils to choose one of the jobs in pop music and talk to their partner about.

- Ask questions with the whole class: *What do you do? (I'm a video director. I make a story board. Then ...)*

 What do these people do? Read and match.

- Ask pupils to read and match the jobs with what the people do. Check the answers with the whole class.

Key

2 A sound engineer looks after the sound equipment.
3 A lighting engineer looks after the lighting.
4 A roadie carries all the band's equipment.
5 A record producer puts the songs together to make an album.
6 A video director makes videos to go with the songs.

Ending the lesson

Game: What's my job?

- Ask a pupil to choose one of the jobs in pop music. The others must find out what it is by asking questions: *Do you play in a band? Do you go on tour?* etc.

Lesson 3

Language	New words and expressions
* interested in	a bit, especially, meter, crazy about, poster, globe, binoculars, astronomy

* = *new language*

Beginning the lesson

- Ask pupils to tell the class about their favorite kinds of music.

 What is Karen interested in?

Look and say.

- Look at the picture of Karen's room with the whole class and identify the objects in it: *posters, globe, cassette, binoculars, astronomy*, etc.

- Ask pupils to talk about what Karen is interested in, working in pairs.

 Play the cassette for pupils to check their answers.

Tapescript and key

Boy: What are you interested in, Karen?
Karen: Um ... I'm interested in a lot of things.
Boy: How about sports?
Karen: Well, I like watching football on TV.
Boy: Do you play any sports?
Karen: Yes, a few, but I'm not very interested in sports.
Boy: How about music?
Karen: I love pop music. I listen to my cassettes all the time.
Boy: Do you like computer games?
Karen: No. I'm not interested in computers.
Boy: Are you interested in traveling?
Karen: Yes! I want to go to Africa. I want to see the animals there, especially the elephants.
Boy: Are you interested in animals? Do you have any pets?
Karen: I love animals. I have a dog. And I have some fish.
Boy: Are you interested in airplanes?
Karen: Mm ... I'm more interested in spaceships. I'm a member of the astronomy club at school. I have some bincoulars to look at the stars. And I've made a model spaceship.

- Ask questions with the whole class. *Is Karen interested in football? (Yes.) How do you know? (She has a poster on her wall.)* etc.

- Look at the interest meter with the whole class. Teach *meter* and *crazy about.*

 Play the model dialog on the cassette. Pupils listen and repeat.

- Ask pupils to talk about their own interests with their partners, making sentences from the interest meter: *I'm crazy about (movies); I'm very interested in (space); I'm interested in (animals); I'm not very interested in (computers); I'm not interested in (football).*

 ## Write the name of the instruments.

- Ask pupils to write the names of the instruments. Check the answers with the whole class. (*Piano, flute, saxophone, guitar, trumpet, recorder.*)

 Play the cassette, pausing for pupils to write the numbers beside the pictures of the instruments.

Key

1 flute **2** trumpet **3** saxophone **4** recorder **5** guitar **6** piano

 Play the song on the cassette. Pupils listen and write down the instruments they can hear.

- Check the answers with the whole class.

Key

Guitar and piano.

 ## How do you pronounce the letter U in these words? Write the words in the correct box.

- Pupils work in pairs to write the words in the correct boxes.

 Play the cassette for pupils to check their answers.

Tapescript and key

Music, Tuesday, museum, united, use, huge, usually.
Drum, trumpet, under, rubber, lunch, bus, hungry.

Ending the lesson

- Pupils can draw their own interest meters, showing where different hobbies and activities come, and talk about them to the whole class.

Lesson 4

Language	New words and expressions
* *Sequencing* *Present continuous*	first, then, next, after that, finally, untroubled, free, dream, war

* = *new language*

Beginning the lesson

 Teach the song *New World* in the usual way.

 ## A video storyboard

- Look at the storyboard for the song with the whole class. Teach *first, then, next, after that, finally, untroubled, free, dream,* and *war.*

 Play the model dialog on the cassette. Pupils listen and repeat.

- Pupils talk about the storyboard in pairs, saying what is happening in each picture.

- Check the answers with the whole class.

Key

First the singer is playing a guitar.
Then some children are running through a field.
Next a man and a woman are walking along a road.

After that some children are playing soccer.
Then some children are having a picnic.
Finally the man and the woman are singing with
the children.

- Discuss with the class how the pictures match
the words of the song.

 ### Make your own video

Make a storyboard for your favorite song.

 Ask pupils in pairs or groups to design their own
storyboards for a song they know, e.g. one of the
songs from the Popcorn cassette.

- Pupils describe their storyboards to the rest of
the class.

- Groups could play the song for their video and
act out the scenes on the storyboard.

 ### Who's your favorite pop star?
Fill in his/her details here.

- Ask pupils if they already know any of the
details about their favorite pop stars. Ask them
how they can find out the information they need.

- If the information is not readily available, pupils
can complete the Pop File for homework.

 ### Make your own pop cassette.
Put these sentences in the right order.

- Ask pupils to read the sentences, then number
them in the right order.

- Check the answers with the whole class.

Key

From top to bottom the order should be:
2, 5, 4, 7, 3, 1, 6.

Ending the lesson

- Pupils can follow the instructions in exercise F
and record their own song.

Project idea

- Pupils can do a project on the history of one kind
of music, or a biography of a favorite performer.
They could also find out about how musical
instruments are made.

Assessment activity

- Ask pupils to write questions for the following
answers:

1 My favorite music is reggae.
2 They look after the lighting at pop concerts.
3 I'd like to learn to play the saxophone.
4 No, I'm not very interested in astronomy.
5 In a recording studio.

Language review 4

Lesson 1

> **Language**
> *Present perfect*

Beginning the lesson

- Ask pupils about things they have done today: *Have you played any games? Have you had your lunch? Have you listened to the radio?* etc.

 **Present perfect**

- Look at the dialog (*Now you can ...*) and ask pupils to explain in L1 how the present perfect is used.
- Play the model dialog on the cassette. Pupils listen and repeat.
- Look at the file cards with the class. Ask them to tell you what they notice about regular past participles (they are formed like regular simple past verbs with *-ed*).

PB 56 ex 1 **Things to do**

 1 Play the cassette. Pupils listen and answer the questions.

Tapescript

Have you had your breakfast?
Have you cleaned your teeth?
Have you played tennis today?
Have you listened to the radio?
Have you watched TV?
Have you drawn a picture?

Play the cassette again. Pupils listen and repeat the questions.

- Pupils practice asking and answering the questions in pairs.

2 In pairs or groups, pupils talk about the things they have done today. Ask pupils to report their answers to the class.

3 Pupils make their own file cards, using different verbs. Ask them to work in pairs to look for more present perfect verbs in the Pupils' Book.

Ending the lesson

Game: What have we done today?

The first player says: *I've (played basketball) today.* The next player adds another activity to the list: *Maria's played basketball and I've painted a picture today.* The game continues around the class. The activities listed need not, of course, be true.

Lesson 2

> **Language**
> *Present Perfect*

Beginning the lesson

Play the game *What have we done today?*

AB 44 ex A **Complete the table.**

- Ask pupils to find the missing verbs to complete the table.
- Check the answers with the class. Ask pupils to tell you which verbs are regular and which are irregular.

Key

verb	simple past	past participle
play	played	played
give	gave	given
take	took	taken
make	made	made
eat	ate	eaten
do	did	done
come	came	come
ride	rode	ridden

 **Tina is in Florida. Don is talking to her on the phone. Write Don's questions.**

- Ask pupils, working in pairs, to look at the answers and write the questions.
- Check the answers with the whole class.

Key

Have you done lots of interesting things?
Have you swum in the ocean?

Have you taken any photos?
Have you seen any alligators?

- Pupils can practice the conversation in pairs. Ask them to think of some more questions and answers to add to the conversation.

 Complete Tina's postcard to Don.

- Ask pupils to use the information from exercise B to write the postcard.
- Check the answers with the whole class.

Key

I'm having a wonderful time! I've done lots of interesting things. I've swum in the ocean every day. I've taken some photos. I've seen lots of alligators.

 Carl has made a list of things to do on Saturday. Listen and put a check beside the things he's done and a cross beside the things he hasn't done.

- Read the list with the class.

 Play the cassette. Pupils put checks and crosses beside the things on the list.

Tapescript and key

Girl: What's this, Carl?
Carl: It's my list of things to do today.
Girl: Have you done all of these things?
Carl: Er ... no.
Girl: Let me see. "Write a letter to Aunt Susan." Have you written a letter to Aunt Susan?
Carl: Um ... no, I haven't.
Girl: I see. Well, have you bought a notebook?
Carl: No.
Girl: Have you finished your science project?
Carl: Yes, I have. It took a long time, too. I was too busy to do some other things.
Girl: Really? So have you practiced your guitar?
Carl: No, I haven't.
Girl: Have you phoned Gina?
Carl: Yes, I have. And I've phoned Sam, too.
Girl: And have you fixed your bike?
Carl: No, but I've played my new computer game. Would you like to try it?

 Play the cassette again. Pupils listen and write down the things that Carl has done which are not on the list.

Key

1 He's phoned Sam.
2 He's played his new computer game.

- Pupils ask and answer questions about the things Carl has and hasn't done (Has he bought a notebook? No, he hasn't.).

Ending the lesson

- Ask pupils each to write an instruction to do something in the class e.g. *open the window. Put your book under your chair.* Collect the instructions and ask pupils, in turn, to take an instruction, perform the action and ask the class: *What have I done?* The others answer: *You've (opened the window).*

Lesson 3

Language	New words and expressions
Present perfect	scar, cheek, false teeth, make-up, eyebrows

Beginning the lesson

- Discuss in L1 how people can change their appearance in movies. Ask pupils to tell you about examples in movies and TV programs they have seen.

 Skills review 4: Speaking

- Look at the pictures of George Jackson with the class. Teach the new vocabulary: *scar, cheek, false teeth, make-up* and *eyebrows.*
- Ask pupils, working in pairs, to talk about the changes made to George's appearance.
- Check the answers with the class, asking questions: *What's happened to George's hair? What has Sally done? Who's drawn lines on George's face?* etc.

PB 57 ex 5 Things to do

1 Ask pupils to draw pictures of George as Jake the pirate and write sentences about him.

Key

1 Sally has made a wig with long hair.
2 Peter has painted a scar on George's cheek.
3 Sally has made some false teeth.
4 George has grown a beard.
5 Peter has drawn lines on George's face.
6 Peter has put brown make-up on George's face.
7 Sally has made some false eyebrows.

2 Ask pupils to draw themselves as characters in the movie "Jake the Pirate". Pupils then talk about their pictures in pairs or groups.

Ending the lesson

• Ask pupils to show the class the pictures of themselves as movie characters. What changes have they made?

Optional Lesson 4

Language
Present perfect

Beginning the lesson

• Ask pupils to work in pairs or groups to find out and write down the past participles of as many verbs as possible. Ask them to tell the rest of the class.

More practice with the present perfect

1 Ask pupils to imagine that they are having a very special vacation. Ask them to write a postcard telling all the things they have done. Pupils can make the whole postcard, drawing a picture of the place on one side and writing the message on the other.

2 Ask pupils to think of ways to change the classroom, and, working in pairs or groups, to draw their design and tell the class or write down, the changes they have made e.g. *We've moved the bookshelves. We've painted the walls blue.*

3 **Game: What's different?**

Divide the class into teams. Send one member of each team out of the classroom. Meanwhile, change five things in the classroom, e.g. open a window or move a piece of furniture. Invite the team members back into the classroom. The first one to spot and describe a change (You've opened the window!) wins a point for his or her team. (Introduce a time limit, e.g. one minute, to guess and then give clues to add "pace" to the activity.)

Unit 13 Can we speak to Rick Morell, please?

Background information

Kate, Sam, Marina and Dan now think they know where Jake Jones, the pirate, buried his treasure. It is at the home of Rick Morell, the pop star, in the desert. They have decided to go to Mexico City to look for Rick and ask him to help them to find the treasure.

Lesson 1

Language	New words and expressions
Asking for permission Can I/we ...? can (ability)	head for, vulture, nest, sunhat, shovel, pick, tape measure, flashlight, metal detector

Beginning the lesson

- Ask pupils to tell you about the story so far. Ask: *Where are Kate and Sam going? Why?*

 Can we speak to Rick Morell, please?

- Open Pupils' Books at page 58 and discuss the story. Ask pupils to tell you what the characters in the pictures are doing.

 Listen to the cassette. Pupils follow the story in the Pupils' Book.

- Ask questions about the story: *Did they speak to Rick Morell in Mexico City? What did they do next?* etc.

 Play the cassette again, pausing for pupils to repeat.

 How can Rick Morell help them?

Listen and find the things they need.

- Look at the pictures of the things they need and teach the new vocabulary *sunhat, shovel, pick, tape measure, flashlight* and *metal detector.*

 Play the cassette. Pupils listen and point to the things they need.

Tapescript and key

Rick: I'd love to help you find the treasure. How can I help?

Marina: Well, we came straight here and I'm afraid we don't have any equipment for finding the treasure.
Rick: OK! So what do you need?
Dan: Do you have a compass?
Rick: Yes, I can lend you a compass.
Marina: How about picks and shovels?
Rick: Yes, I can find some of those. And I can help you dig, of course.
Kate: Thanks, Rick.
Dan: We need a long tape measure to measure the ground.
Rick: No problem, Dan. I have one right here.
Marina: It's going to be hot in the desert. How can we keep cool?
Rick: Well, I have lots of hats we can wear. They'll keep the sun off our heads and I can supply lots of water for us to drink.
Sam: Will it take us a long time to find the treasure?
Rick: Maybe it will, Sam. But we can work at night with flashlights. I have lots of those.
Dan: Well, thanks, Rick. That's very helpful. We can start digging tomorrow.
Rick: Wait a minute, Dan. I have something else we can use. Look!
Kate: What is it?
Sam: I know. It's a metal detector. That's going to be very useful.

- Check the answers by asking the questions to the whole class: *They want to measure the ground. What do they need?* etc.

 Play the cassette again. Pupils listen and repeat.

 Can you find six mistakes in these notes about the story in the Pupils' Book? Draw circles around the mistakes and write the correct words.

- Ask pupils, working on their own or in pairs, to circle the incorrect words and write the correct words.

- Check the answers with the class.

Key

1 pop star **2** Mexico City **3** big black car **4** car
5 in the desert **6** wanted to help them

Ending the lesson

• Play a game of *I spy* using the pictures on pages 58 and 59 of the Pupils' Book: *I spy with my little eye something beginning with ...* etc.

Lesson 2

Language	New words and expressions
Can I ...?	No, I'm sorry ...
Present perfect	cream, pills

Beginning the lesson

• Practice asking permission to do things: *Can I borrow your book, please? Can I open the window, please?* Encourage pupils to ask similar questions.

 Read and match.

• Ask pupils to read and match the questions and answers.

• Check the answers by asking the questions. Pupils respond.

Key

2 Can I play soccer with you, please? No, I'm sorry, I've broken my leg.
3 Can I have my pens back, please? No, I'm sorry, I've lost them.
4 Can I have some chocolate, please? No, I'm sorry, I've eaten it.
5 Can I borrow your bike, please? No, I'm sorry, I've sold it.

• Pupils practice asking and answering the questions in pairs.

 Look at these four houses. Can you say who lives there?

• Ask pupils to work in pairs to look at the pictures and decide whose houses they are.

• Check the answers with the whole class, by asking questions: *Whose house is this? (An explorer's.) What can you see in the room? What can you see in the closet? Why does she need insect bite cream?* etc.

• Pupils write sentences about the rooms in the pictures, following the example.

Key

I think an explorer lives here. She is interested in traveling and climbing. She needs travel pills because she travels a lot and insect bite cream because there are lots of insects in the rainforest.

I think a stunt artist lives here. She is interested in keeping in shape and movies. She needs a helmet to protect her head and a first-aid kit because her job is very dangerous.

I think this is an astronomer's room. He is interested in the planets and stars. He needs a hat and scarf because it is cold outside at night. He needs binoculars to look at the sky at night.

Pupils draw pictures of their own rooms and talk about them to their friends.

 Ask pupils to describe their friends' rooms to the rest of the class: *This is Maria's room. I think she's interested in music, because she has a guitar. There's a big closet. She needs a big closet because she has a lot of clothes.*

Ending the lesson

Game: Asking permission.

• Ask pairs of pupils to write questions and answers, like those in exercise B in the Activity Book, on separate pieces of paper. Distribute these around the class. Pupils with questions read them aloud and the pupils with the answers respond, until all the questions and answers have been matched.

Lesson 3

Language	New words and expressions
Where's ... ?	over there, playing field
Prepositions	Can you tell me the way to ...?
Can I/we ...?	paintbrush, park keeper
want to	ice cream van, picnic area

Beginning the lesson

• Review prepositions. Ask: *What's in the middle of the table? What's next to ...? What's between ...?* etc. Ask pupils to ask each other *Where* questions about things in the classroom.

 Where are these things?

Find these things in the picture of the park. Talk to your friend.

Ask pupils in pairs to find the things in the box in the picture of the park. Play the model dialog for pupils to listen and repeat.

• Check the answers with the whole class by asking questions: *Where's the duck?* etc.

Key

The duck is in the middle of the lake.
The girl near the ice cream van is holding the ice cream cone.
The man in the phone box is holding the phone.
The ball is in the middle of the picnic.
The pen is on the picnic table.
The paintbrush is on the grass, next to the two children who are painting.
The boat is in the middle of the lake.

- Look at the picture of the park with the whole class. Teach vocabulary: *playing field, picnic area, ice cream van, park keeper.*

 Asking for things

Who's talking? Listen and point to the people in the picture.

- Ask pupils to listen to the conversations on the cassette and find the people in the picture.

 Play the cassette, pausing for pupils to say where the people who are talking are and what they are doing. Ask questions: *Who's speaking? Where are they? What are they doing?*

Tapescript and key

Narrator: One.
Boy: Can you tell me the way to the lake, please?
Woman: It's over there, next to the trees past the picnic area.
(It's the boy and the woman at the front of the picture. The boy is holding a toy boat.)
Narrator: Two.
Girl: Can I borrow your pen, please?
Boy: Yes, here you are.
(It's the girl and the boy in the picnic area. They are writing letters.)
Narrator: Three.
Man: Can we play soccer here?
Woman: No, you can't. You must go to the playing field.
(It's the man with the children and the park keeper. They have a soccer ball.)
Narrator: Four.
Girl: Can we have our picnic here, please, Mom?
Woman: Yes, this looks like a good place.
(It's the woman and the children near the picnic area. They are carrying some picnic things.)
Narrator: Five.
Man: Can I speak to Mrs Watson please?
Woman: Yes, this is Mrs Watson speaking.
(It's the man in the phone box. He's making a phone call.)

Narrator: Six.
Boy: Can we feed the ducks, please?
Girl: Yes, OK then.
(It's the girl and the little boy beside the lake. The little boy has some food for the ducks.)

- Ask questions with *want to* + infinitive: *What does the little boy beside the lake want to do?* (He wants to feed the ducks.) etc.

 Play the conversations on the cassette again. Pupils listen and repeat.

Pupils ask and answer questions following the model dialog. They should think of conversations for the other people in the park.

- Check the answers with the whole class, asking pairs of pupils to repeat their conversations.

Key

Can I borrow your paintbrush, please? Yes, of course.
Can I go on a boat, please? Yes, of course./No, I'm sorry, we can't.
Can I have an ice cream cone, please? Yes, of course.

Ending the lesson

- Play the asking permission game again, with new questions and answers.

Lesson 4

Language	New words and expressions
Present perfect	scorpion, camel, eagle
Can we ...?	
Past simple	
Materials needed	
dice or spinners and counters for playing the game	

Beginning the lesson

- Pupils practice asking permission to do things e.g. *Can I open the window, please? Can I borrow your ruler, please?*

PB 61 ex 4 **Follow the parrot**

Game.

- Pupils play the game in pairs. They must ask the people they meet for help as they follow the parrot.

- After finishing the game, ask pupils to repeat what they asked.

Key

Mr. Green, can we borrow your ladder, please?
Can we have two tickets to the park, please?
Can we go to the island in your canoe, please?
Can we borrow your canoe, please?
Can we borrow the key for the shed, please?
Can we use your binoculars, please?
Mrs. Smith, can we come into your yard, please?

- Pupils practice the dialogs in pairs, with responses (*Yes, of course. Here it is.*) etc.
- Pupils tell the story again in the past tense, including all the things they did when they followed the parrot.

Check the answers with the whole class.

Key

First we saw it outside Mr. Green's store. We borrowed his ladder but the parrot flew away. Then we saw it on the bus. We bought two tickets to the park, but we didn't catch the parrot on the bus. After that we saw it on an island in the lake. We borrowed a canoe from our teacher, but the parrot flew away again. It flew into a shed. The shed was locked. We borrowed the key from the park keeper, but the parrot escaped. Then it flew to the middle of the park. We borrowed some binoculars from a girl and found it, but it flew away again. Finally, we saw it in Mrs. Smith's yard. We went into Mrs. Smith's yard and caught the parrot.

 Write the names of the animals.

- Ask pupils to identify the animals they know and write their names in the boxes. Teach the new words: *scorpion, camel* and *eagle.*

 Ask pupils in pairs to decide where the animals live then play the cassette for pupils to check their answers.

Tapescript and key

Boy: Which animals live in the desert?
Girl: Mmm, let me see. Scorpions live in the desert, and vultures can live in the desert and er ... oh, yes, camels live in the desert, too.

Boy: Do tigers live in the desert?
Girl: No, they live in the rainforest. Orangutans live in the forest, too. They live in the rainforests of southeast Asia. And parrots live in the rainforest, too.
Boy: Which animals live in the mountains?
Girl: Eagles live in the mountains. And sheep live in the mountains. Which animals live in towns?
Boy: Pigeons live in towns and cats live in towns. I have a cat in my house. And ducks can live in towns, too. There are some ducks in the park.
Girl: And foxes can live in towns, too.

- Check the answers with the whole class.

Ending the lesson

Game: Guess the animal

- Pupils think of an animal and the others must guess it by asking questions: *Does it live in towns? Does it eat meat? Is it bigger than a cat? Does it have a long tail?* etc. The pupils can only answer *Yes* or *No.*

Project idea

- Deserts: Pupils could find out more about the world's deserts: Where are they? What kind of animals live in the desert? How can people survive in the desert?

Assessment activity

- Ask pupils to write questions to go with the following answers:

1 Yes, of course. It's in my backpack.
2 No, I'm sorry. My computer's broken.
3 There they are. They're in the middle of the playing field.
4 They live in the desert.
5 I'm interested in astronomy.

Unit 14   A trip around the world

Lesson 1

Language	New words and expressions
Past simple	tortoise, coach, dogsled, continent, Europe, Africa, Australia, South America, North America, Antarctica, Asia, journey, by sea, bullet train

Beginning the lesson

- Talk to pupils about everyday transportation. Ask: *How do you come to school? Do you come by bus? Who walks to school? How do your parents go to work?* etc.

A trip around the world

- Open pupils' Books at page 62 and ask questions about the pictures: *Where are the people in the pictures? What are they doing?* Teach the new word *tortoise.*

- Ask pupils to find the places in the photos on a map of the world.

- Check the answers with the whole class. Teach *continent* and the names of the continents. Ask: *Where's Alaska? (It's in North America.)* etc.

Transportation

Find the different kinds of transportation.

- Teach the new words *coach* and *dog sled.* Ask pupils to find the vehicles in the pictures on pages 62 and 63.

- Ask pupils to match the transportation to the countries, following the model dialog on the cassette.

- Talk about the transportation with the whole class: *Where do they travel by dogsled? (Alaska.) Do people use dogsleds anywhere else? (Greenland, Canada, Antarctica),* etc.

How did they travel?

Listen to Zoe and Paul. They are talking about their trip. Point to the transportation they used.

- Ask pupils to make a list of the places Zoe and Paul visited. (Alaska, Egypt, U.S.A., Thailand, Japan, Ecuador, the Galapagos Islands.)

- Play the cassette. Pupils listen and write the order in which Zoe and Paul visited the places: *Alaska (5), Egypt (1),* etc.

Tapescript and key

Zoe: On the 8th of May we went by sea from New York to Egypt. We saw the pyramids and we had a ride on a camel. Then we traveled up the Nile river by sailing boat.

Paul: Then we flew from Egypt to Thailand. We traveled to a village in the north of Thailand by bus. It took us a long time to reach the village, because the bus went quite slowly.

Zoe: We left Thailand by airplane, and flew to Japan. We traveled by train in Japan. It was a very fast train called the bullet train.

Paul: Then we left Japan and flew across the Pacific Ocean to Ecuador. We went to the Galapagos Islands. We traveled among the islands in a small island canoe.

Zoe: Then we flew to San Francisco in the United States. We drove all the way up the west coast to Alaska by car. When we were in Alaska we went to see some friends by dogsled.

Paul: From Alaska we flew to New York.

- Ask pupils to listen again and find the transportation that Zoe and Paul used in their trip.

- Check the answers as you ask questions about the trip: *When did they leave New York? Where did they go? How did they travel?*

- Teach the new vocabulary: *by sea, bullet train.*

-  Play the cassette again, pausing for pupils to repeat.

- Pupils talk about Zoe and Paul's trip in pairs.

- Ask pupils in pairs to plan a trip around the world.

Ending the lesson

- Ask pairs of pupils to explain their trip to the rest of the class.

Lesson 2

Language	New words and expressions
Past simple	tennis court, wind power, gas engine, magic
How ...?	diesel engine, human power
by + transportation	sail buggy, windsurfer, tractor, sailing ship, magic carpet, broomstick

Beginning the lesson

- Ask questions about transportation and review times: *How do you come to school? How did you come here this morning? What time did you leave home? When did you arrive here? How long did it take?*

 Can you find the names of eleven kinds of transportation in the word square? Write labels for the pictures.

- Pupils work in pairs to find the names in the word square. Check the answers with the class.

Key

1 helicopter **2** motorbike **3** airplane **4** truck
5 bus **6** ship **7** boat **8** car **9** sled **10** train
11 canoe

 Four friends played tennis together last week. Listen and fill in the table.

 Play the cassette, pausing for pupils to fill in the details on the table.

Tapescript

Gina: Hi! I'm Gina. I went by car. My brother drove me. We left home at eight-thirty and I arrived at the tennis court at ten o'clock.

James: My name's James. I traveled by bus. I arrived there at ten after ten. I left home at nine-fifty.

Fred: Hello. I'm Fred. I went to the tennis court by train. I left home at twenty to ten and I arrived at eight minutes after ten.

Roberta: I'm Roberta and I went by bike. I left my house at nine-fifteen and I arrived at the tennis court at five to ten.

 Play the cassette again for pupils to check their answers. Then check the answers with the class.

Key

	went by	left home at	arrived at	How long did it take?
Gina	car	8:30	10:00	1 hour 30 mins
James	bus	9:50	10:10	20 mins
Fred	train	9:40	10:08	28 mins
Roberta	bike	9:15	9:55	40 mins

- Pupils can practice talking about the table in pairs: *Who traveled by bike? How long did it take Roberta to go to the tennis court?* etc.

 Match the kinds of transportation to the power they use.

- Ask pupils to identify the types of transportation in the pictures. Teach *sail buggy, wind surfer, tractor, sailing ship, magic carpet* and *broomstick.*

- Teach the words in the box (*wind power, gas engine, diesel engine, human power* and *magic*).

- Ask pupils to work out in pairs what kind of power the different kinds of transportation use.

- Check the answers with the whole class.

Key

The truck, the train, the bus and the tractor use diesel engines.
The windsurfer, the sailing ship and the sail buggy use wind power.
The bike uses human power.
The broomstick and the magic carpet use magic.

- Ask pupils to discuss in pairs or groups which kinds of transportation are clean and which are dirty.

Key

Green – the windsurfer, the sailing ship, the sail buggy, the magic carpet, the broomstick and the bicycle.
Red – the truck, the car, the motorbike, the train, the bus and the tractor.

Ending the lesson

Game: Round the world trip

- The first player starts by saying: *We went to Australia by airplane.* The next player continues, adding a new destination and means of transportation: *We went to Australia by airplane then we went to Indonesia by canoe.* The game continues around the class.

Lesson 3

Language	New words and expressions
Future with *will*	solar power, personal, sidewalk

Beginning the lesson

- Ask questions about transportation: *Can you go from here to New York by train? What is the best/easiest/fastest way to go to New York?* etc.

 Travel in the future

Look at the pictures and talk to your friend.

- Look at the pictures of the different kinds of transportation. Teach *solar power, personal* and *sidewalk.*
 Play the model dialog on the cassette. Pupils listen and repeat.
- Ask pupils to look at the pictures in pairs, and decide if they think children will use any of these kinds of transportation in the future.
- Discuss the transportation of the future with the class. Ask pupils to explain why the different kinds of transportation illustrated would or would not work.
- Ask pupils, working in pairs or groups, to design their own methods of transportation for the future. Ask them to show their pictures to the rest of the class and explain how their inventions work.
- Ask pupils to write about their inventions, giving their inventions names, saying what kind of power they use, and explaining how they work and what their advantages are.

Ending the lesson

- Play the game: *Round the world trip* from Lesson 2.

Lesson 4

Language	New words and expressions
going to	insect spray, snorkel, flippers, scuba equipment, stick, straight, wire, lid, thread, edge, rod

Materials needed
cardboard, straws, thin stick or wire, lids, glue, scissors, sticky tape, thread

Beginning the lesson

- Ask pupils about a round the world trip: *Would you like to go around the world? Where would you like to go? What would you like to do? What would you like to see?*

PB 65 ex 4 What are you going to take?

- Look at the list of things to take with the whole class and teach the new vocabulary: *insect spray, snorkel, flippers,* and *scuba equipment.*
- Play the model dialog on the cassette. Pupils listen and repeat.
- Pupils discuss what they are going to take in pairs. Remind them that their luggage must not weigh more than 20 kg.
- Talk to the whole class about what they are going to take: *Are you going to take a swimsuit? Where are you going to swim? Will you need any party clothes?* Elicit answers like *I won't need ...* and *... too heavy ... I'd like to ... but ...*
- Ask pupils if there is anything else they would like to take that is not on the list e.g. *camera, diary.*

AB 51 ex D Make a sail buggy.

- Read the instructions with the whole class and teach the new vocabulary: *stick, straight, wire, lid, thread, edge* and *rod.*
- Pupils make the sail buggy in pairs or groups, following the instructions.
- Ask pairs or groups of pupils to tell you about the sail buggies they have made: *What did you do first? We stuck the straws ...* etc.

Ending the lesson

- Ask pupils in pairs to try to remember as many as possible of the things on the list of luggage on page 65 of the Pupils' Book, without looking at their books.

Project ideas

- Transportation: Pupils can find out about different kinds of transportation in their own country or area. They could, for example, do a census of the traffic passing their school, counting the cars, buses, bicycles etc. that go past in a ten minute period.
- Travel plans: Pupils can plan a trip they would like to make e.g. a trip around the world or a continent. They could research an itinerary of routes, transportation and stopovers and make a list of what they would need to take e.g. passports, visas, medicine, clothes, currency etc.

Assessment activity

- Ask pupils to write answers to the following
  questions:

  1 How can you travel from New York to Paris?
  2 How did you come to school today?
  3 How will children travel to school in the
     future?
  4 What kind of power does a bus use?
  5 How long does it take you to come to school?

Unit 15 Buried treasure

Background information

Kate, Sam, Marina and Dan have traveled to Mexico to meet the pop star, Rick Morell. They believe that Jake Jones's treasure is buried somewhere near Rick's house in the desert. Rick has agreed to help them to look for the treasure.

Lesson 1

Language	New words and expressions
First conditional	believe, pace, bend

Beginning the lesson

- Ask pupils questions about the story so far: *Where are Kate and Sam? Why have they gone there? What are they going to do?*

PB 66  **Buried treasure**

- Open Pupils' Books at page 66 and discuss the story. Ask pupils to tell you what they think the characters in the pictures are doing.
- Listen to the cassette. Pupils follow the story in the Pupils' Book.
- Teach the new vocabulary: *believe, pace* and *bend* as you ask questions about the story.
- Play the cassette again, pausing for pupils to repeat.

AB 52 ex A **Read and draw on the map.**

- Ask pupils to work in pairs to read the sentences and complete the drawing of the map.
- Check the answers with the class.

Key

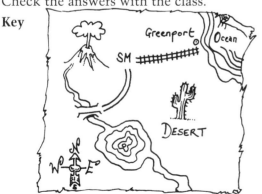

- Ask questions about the map: *Where does the road go? Where's the desert?* etc.

- Ask pupils to think of a place to hide the treasure on their maps. Pupils tell their partners where their treasure is hidden. Tell pupils they can draw other features on the map if they wish.

Ending the lesson

- Ask pupils to describe to the rest of the class where on the map they have hidden their treasure.

Lesson 2

Language	New words and expressions
First conditional	computer disks, messy

Beginning the lesson

- Ask questions about the classroom: *What'll you find if you open this box? Will you find any pencils if you look in here?* etc.

PB 67 ex 1 **Sam's room**

Sam's room is very messy. He can't find any of his things. Listen and find out where they are.

- Look at the picture of Sam's room. Teach *computer disk* and *messy*. Ask pupils if they can see any of the things that Sam has lost.
- Play the cassette, pausing for pupils to answer the questions.

  Tapescript and key

  Girl: Where's Sam's shoe?
  Boy: It's on top of the closet.
  Girl: And where are his sunglasses?
  Boy: They're on the floor. They're under his hat.
  Girl: Where's his camera?
  Boy: It's behind his computer.
  Girl: And the computer disks? Where are they?
  Boy: They're under the bed.
  Girl: Where's his diary?
  Boy: It's under the pillow on the floor.
  Girl: Where's his dictionary?
  Boy: It's on the floor, too. It's behind the chair.

- Check the answers by asking questions with the whole class.
- Play the model sentence on the cassette. Pupils listen and repeat.

74

- Pupils talk about the things in the box in pairs. They can also write sentences.

 Don and Jack are on a camping trip. Jack can't find anything. Listen and draw lines.

- Ask pupils to listen to the cassette and draw lines from the things to the places where they are packed.

 Play the cassette, pausing for pupils to draw the lines.

Tapescript and key

Jack: Don! I can't find the matches.
Don: The matches? If you look in the black backpack you'll find them.
Jack: Thanks. Er ... Where are the sheets?
Don: They're in the long gray bag.
Jack: Oh, yes. I've found them. Now I can't find the knives and forks.
Don: If you open the flat gray box, you'll find the knives and forks.
Jack: Will I find the cups in the flat gray box?
Don: The cups? No, they're in that square white box.
Jack: Thanks. Now then, the can opener. Where's the can opener, Don?
Don: You'll find it if you look inside the white backpack.
Jack: Here it is. Do you know where the kettle is?
Don: The kettle? Yes, if you look in that tall gray box, you'll find the kettle.
Jack: I've found it. Er ... Don?
Don: Yes.
Jack: Have you found the tent?
Don: The tent? Oh no! I think we've forgotten to pack the tent!

- Check the answers by asking questions: *Where are the matches?* etc.

 Play the cassette again, pausing for pupils to listen and repeat.

Ending the lesson

- Divide the class into groups. Ask one group to hide something in the classroom. The other groups must ask questions to find it: *Will we find it if look under the table?* etc. The first group to find the object wins a point and takes a turn to hide the next thing.

Lesson 3

Language	New words and expressions
First conditional	grab, slip, pool, cart, store detective

Beginning the lesson

- Ask pupils to give instructions to find things in the classroom.

PB 68 ex 2 **In the supermarket**

Look at the picture and match the sentences.

- Look at the picture with the class and teach the new vocabulary: *grab, slip, pool, cart* and *store detective.*
- Ask pupils, working in pairs, to look at the picture and match the sentences.
- Check the answers with the whole class.

Key

If he grabs the box of cookies the whole pile will fall down.
If he steps in the pool of oil he'll slip and fall down.
If she buys three packs of soap she'll get a free hat.
If he steals the turkey the store detective will catch him.
If she eats all the ice cream on her own she'll get sick.
If they race their carts the manager will throw them out.

 Play the model dialog on the cassette. Pupils listen and repeat.

- Pupils talk about the picture in pairs, following the model dialog.

AB 53 ex C **Match the sentences.**

- Ask pupils to look at the picture and match the sentences, working in pairs.
- Check the answers with the whole class.

Key

1 If you go into the library you'll find lots of books.
2 If you buy ice cream you'll get a surprise gift.
3 If you go to the movie theater you'll see a science fiction movie.
4 If you go into the park you'll see a cycle race today.

- Pupils can continue asking questions in pairs: *What'll happen if you cross the road?* etc.

Ending the lesson

• Ask pupils about things that are happening in their area: *If you go to the movie theater this week you'll see ...* etc.

Lesson 4

> **Language**
> *Past simple*
> How long ...?
> How deep ...?

Beginning the lesson

• Ask pupils about the story: *Where did Jake Jones bury the treasure? Did Kate and Sam know where the treasure was? How did they know? Who's helping them? What must they do to find the treasure?*

 Digging for treasure

Listen and answer the questions.

• Look at the pictures and read the questions with the class.

 Play the cassette, pausing for pupils to answer the questions in the Pupil's Book.

Tapescript and key

Kate: Hello. Sam and I are recording a diary about our hunt for the treasure.

Sam: We're going to tell you all about what happened.

Kate: We started looking for the treasure at six-thirty in the morning.

Sam: We started early because it's cooler then.

Kate: But it took us quite a long time to find the place where Jake buried the treasure.

Sam: It took us an hour and a half. We started digging at nine-thirty.

Kate: It was hard work digging. The ground was very hard, and we had to dig carefully.

Sam: Dan said anything we found was important, even if it wasn't treasure.

Kate: And we did find something.

Sam: It was 65 centimeters under the ground.

Kate: It was a button. It was made of silver. Dan said it was made in the seventeenth century.

Sam: Soon after that, at quarter to twelve, we stopped digging and had a rest.

Kate: We were exhausted. We each drank a whole bottle of water.

Sam: We had a swim in Rick's pool, then we started digging again in the afternoon. And

we found something. It was three meters deep in the ground.

Kate: It look like boxes made of wood and metal.

Sam: I'm sure it's the treasure. What do you think?

• Ask questions about the story: *Why did they start digging early? Who do you think the silver button belonged to? Why did they drink a lot of water?* etc.

 Play the model dialog on the cassette. Pupils listen and repeat.

• Pupils discuss what they think Kate and Sam will do with the treasure in pairs or in groups. Ask pupils to tell the rest of the class what they think.

 Some treasure hunters are going to dig for treasure here. Look at the diagram and write answers to the questions.

• Look at the diagram with the class. Ask pupils to tell you what they can see under the ground (a wheel, a bottle, some coins, a box, a knife, a skeleton).

• Ask pupils to read the questions and write the answers in pairs.

• Check the answers with the class.

Key

1 They'll find the wheel, the coins, the knife and maybe the box if they use a metal detector.
2 If they dig for one meter they'll find the wheel, the bottle and the coins.
3 They'll find five things before they find the skeleton.
4 They'll dig for three meters to find the skeleton.
5 They'll find the bottle first.

AB 54 ex E **Write questions and answers about the bottle.**

• Pupils work in pairs to write questions and answers about the bottle.

• Check the answers with the class.

Key

1 How tall is the bottle? It is 23 centimeters tall.
2 How heavy is the bottle? It weighs 300 grams.
3 How old is the bottle? It is more than 100 years old.

5 When did they find the bottle? On June 10, 1994.

• Pupils practice asking and answering the questions in pairs.

Ending the lesson

• Ask pupils to tell you about things they have found. *What kind of things can they find on the beach? In the country?* etc.

Project ideas

• Archaeology: Pupils could find out how archaelogists work to discover information about the past.

• Pupils could find out what happens to different materials when they are buried in the earth.

Assessment activity

• Ask pupils to write questions for the following answers:

1 These coins are 200 years old.
2 It was two meters deep.
3 I drank a whole bottle of water.
4 If you eat it all, you'll feel sick.
5 If you look in the closet, you'll find it.

Language review 5

Lesson 1

> **Language**
> *First conditional*

Beginning the lesson

- Ask questions with the first conditional: *What'll happen if it rains this afternoon? What'll you do if you feel hungry after school?*

PB 70 The first conditional

- Look at the dialog (*Now you can ...*). Ask pupils to explain what the sentences mean.
- Play the model dialog on the cassette. Pupils listen and repeat.
- Read the sentences on the file card. Ask pupils to suggest their own similar sentences.

PB 70 Things to do

 1 Explain that pupils will hear Kate and Sam getting ready for a trip. Play the cassette. Pupils listen and repeat.

Tapescript

Kate: If you forget the map ...
Sam: ... we'll get lost.
Kate: If we forget the chocolate ...
Sam: ... we'll feel hungry.
Kate: And if we forget the water ...
Sam: ... we'll be thirsty.
Kate: If we don't hurry ...
Sam: ... we'll miss the bus!
Kate: If we run ...
Sam: ... we'll catch the bus.

2 Ask pupils to work in pairs or groups and make up their own similar dialogs about a trip they are getting ready for. Ask pupils to demonstrate their dialogs for the rest of the class.

3 Pupils make cards with the first conditional for their language files.

Ending the lesson

- Ask questions about the dialog between Kate and Sam: *What'll happen if they forget the map? What'll happen if they don't hurry?* etc.

Lesson 2

> **Language**
> *First conditional*

Beginning the lesson

- Ask pupils to explain (in L1) how first conditional sentences are formed.

PB 55 ex A Five of Gina's friends are hiding in the picture. Listen to Gina and fill in the gaps.

 Play the cassette, pausing for pupils to write the missing words in the gaps.

Tapescript and key

My friends are hiding, but I'll tell you where to find them. Listen.
Do you see that big tree in the middle of the picture? If you go behind the tree you'll find my friend Dale. Then if you climb the tree, you'll see my friend Melanie. She's among the branches.
If you look at the left of the picture, you'll see some rocks. You'll find Kim among the rocks. Then if you turn to the right, you'll see an old shed. If you open the door of the shed you'll find Kevin.
Then you'll find a table if you look at the side of the shed. You'll see Abby if you look under the table.

- Check the answers with the class. Ask questions: *Who will you find if you go behind the tree?* etc.

- Ask pupils, working in pairs, to write the names of Gina's friends beside the places where they are hiding. Check the answers with the class.

- Pupils continue asking and answering questions about Gina's friends: *Where will you find Abby? If you look under the table, you'll find her.*

AB 56 ex B Jack is thinking about his plans for the weekend.

- Write the sentences.

- Ask pupils to look at the pictures. Review the weather vocabulary.

- Pupils write about the pictures in pairs.

- Check the answers with the whole class.

Key

If it's rainy, he'll read a book.
If it's sunny, he'll ride his bike.
If it's windy, he'll fly his kite.
If it's cloudy, he'll go to a movie.
If it's snowy, he'll go skiing.

• Pupils can ask and answer questions about Jack's plans in pairs: *What'll he do if it's rainy?* etc.

Ending the lesson

• Ask pupils to talk about their own plans for the weekend in the same way as in exercise B in the Activity Book.

Lesson 3

Language
First conditional

Beginning the lesson

• Ask pupils about things they can do at a party. *What do they eat? What do they drink?* etc.

PB 71 ## Skills review 5: Listening

• Ask pupils to look at the pictures in pairs, and talk about what they think is happening.

 Play the cassette. Pupils listen and point to the pictures.

Tapescript and key

Boy: What'll happen if Don puts the burgers on the chair?
Girl: The dog'll eat them.
Boy: What'll happen if Susie doesn't see the cat?
Girl: She'll drop the salad.
Boy: What'll happen if the table breaks?
Girl: The birthday cake will fall into the pool.
Boy: What'll happen if Andy eats all the chocolate cake?
Girl: He'll be sick.
Boy: What'll happen if it rains?
Girl: They'll have the party in the house.

• Ask questions about the pictures: *What'll happen if the table breaks?* etc.

 PB 71 ## Things to do

1 Play the cassette. Pupils listen and repeat the questions and answers.
2 Ask pupils to talk about the picture in pairs. Practice the questions and answers with the whole class.
3 Ask pupils to write sentences about the picture e.g. *If Don puts the burgers on the chair the dog will eat them.*

• Check the answers with the class.

Key

If Susie doesn't see the cat she'll drop the salad.
If the table breaks the birthday cake will fall into the pool.
If Andy eats all the chocolate cake he'll be sick.
If it rains they'll have the party in the house.

Ending the lesson

• Ask pupils to make up dialogs with the characters in the picture e.g.

A: Don't put the burgers on the chair, Don!
B: Why not?
A: The dog will eat them.

Optional Lesson 4

Language
First conditional

Beginning the lesson

• Ask questions about finding things in the classroom, and around the school e.g. *Where can I find a ruler?* (If you look in the drawer, you'll find one.).

More practice with the first conditional

1 Pupils work in groups to write clues for a treasure hunt: If you go to ... and open the ... you'll find the first clue. Each group should prepare and hide the clues (outside the classroom if possible) and challenge another group to follow them and find the "treasure" within a given time limit.

2 Ask pupils to work together to think of and write safety or health warnings e.g. *If you don't ride your bike carefully, you'll have an accident. If you eat too much sugar, you'll get fat.*

Unit 16 The end of the story

Background information

Kate and Sam and their friends are getting closer to finding the treasure buried by the pirate Jake Jones. They have been digging all day and at last they have found some boxes with the treasure.

Lesson 1

Language	New words and expressions
going to What ... like?	owl, candlestick, necklace, brooch, earring

Beginning the lesson

- Discuss the story of the treasure. Who buried the treasure? Where is it? Why did Jake bury it? Who did he steal it from?

 PB 72 **The end of the story**

- Open Pupils' Books at page 72 and discuss the story. Ask pupils to tell you what they think is happening in the pictures.

 Listen to the cassette. Pupils follow the story in the Pupils' Book.

- Teach the new vocabulary *owl* and *candlestick* and ask questions about the pictures.

 Play the cassette again, pausing for pupils to repeat.

 PB 73 ex 1 **What was he like?**

- What can you find out about General Delgado? Look at his treasure and answer the questions.

- Ask questions about General Delgado: *Where did Jake steal his treasure? Did the General follow him? What happened?*

- Look at the picture of the General's treasure. Teach the vocabulary *necklace, brooch* and *earring*.

- Ask pupils, working in pairs, to look at the picture and answer the questions.

- Check the answers with the class.

  Key

  Yes, the general was very rich. His son looked like Sam. He used silver candlesticks, cups and plates in his house.

- Ask questions: *How do you know the general was very rich?* (He had a lot of gold coins. He had silver plates, etc.

 AB 57 ex A **Picture crossword. Complete the crossword puzzle with the names of the things in the pictures.**

- Ask pupils to complete the crossword. Check the answers with the class.

  Key

  1 plate **2** earring **3** necklace **4** spade
  5 candlestick **6** cup **7** brooch **8** chest

Ending the lesson

- Ask pupils to imagine that they are going to interview Sam and Kate about finding the treasure. What questions would they like to ask? Ask pupils to role play the interview in pairs or groups.

Lesson 2

Language	New words and expressions
going to	time capsule, including, wrapper, meatballs, copy, comic book, air ticket, footprint, adult

Beginning the lesson

- Discuss time capsules. Explain that the treasure in the story told us something about General Delgado and his family. Explain that a time capsule will show people in the future what life is like now.

 PB 74 ex 2 **Time capsules**

Listen and point to the things in the picture.

- Look at the things in the picture. Ask pupils to tell you what they are. Teach the new vocabulary.

 Play the cassette. Pupils listen and point to the things in the picture.

Tapescript and key

Mandy: Hi! My name's Mandy and these are the things I'm going to put into my time capsule. First, I'm going to put in a photo of me and my family, including our dog, Tiger. Then I'm going to put in a picture of my classroom at school. I'm going to put in a T shirt I got at Disneyland – it's too small for me now. And I'm going to put in a wrapper from my favorite chocolate bar, and a recipe for my favorite food – spaghetti and meatballs. Lastly, I'm going to make a cassette. On one side I'm going to record a message from me and my friends, and on the other side I'm going to record my favorite music program from the radio.

Tom: Hi! I'm Tom. These are all the things I'm going to put in my time capsule. The first thing is a copy of my favorite comic book. Then I'm going to put in a menu from a restaurant in our town. My family goes there quite often. Then I'm going to put in a newspaper. I've drawn a picture of our car to put in the capsule and I've cut out a picture of a bike like mine from a magazine. I'm going to put in a model airplane and an air ticket. I'm also going to put in a model astronaut. Oh, and a picture of my favorite football team.

 Play the model dialog on the cassette. Pupils listen and repeat.

• Pupils talk about the things that Mandy and Tom put into their time capsules. Ask them to write a list of the things.

• Check the answers by asking the questions to the whole class.

 Be a detective. What can you find out from some footprints? Write answers Yes, No or I'm not sure.

• Ask pupils to work in pairs to look at the picture then write answers to the questions. Teach *footprint* and *adult*.

• Check the answers with the whole class.

Key

1 Yes 2 No 3 No 4 Yes 5 No 6 I'm not sure

• Ask questions about the tracks: *How do you know the adult wasn't riding the bicycle?* etc.

Ending the lesson

• Ask pupils to draw tracks and ask each other questions about them (*How many people were there? Were they children or adults?* etc.). You could also dictate situations for pupils to draw

e.g. *Two children walked along a path. A cat walked towards them.*

Lesson 3

Language	New words and expressions
I'd like to Why? because	barbecue, costume party

Beginning the lesson

• Ask pupils if they can remember what Mandy and Tom were going to put in their time capsules. What will the things they chose tell people in the future about them?

 What would you like to put in a time capsule?

Talk to your friend.

• Ask pupils to discuss what they would like to put in a time capsule, and make a list.

 Play the model dialog on the cassette. Pupils listen and repeat.

• Pupils tell each other about the things they would like to put in their time capsules. Ask questions with the whole class.

• Discuss things pupils could put in a capsule which would tell people in the future about their class and their school.

 Don is going to have a party. Listen and complete the invitation.

• Ask pupils to listen to Don talking about the plans for his party and fill in the information on the invitation.

 Play the cassette, pausing for pupils to write the answers.

Tapescript

Don: I'm going to have a party.
Girl: Where's it going to be?
Don: At my house. That's 10, Oak Avenue.
Girl: When's it going to be?
Don: On May 15th.
Girl: Is that a Friday?
Don: No, it's a Saturday.
Girl: What time?
Don: It's going to start at six o'clock.
Girl: Are you going to have things to eat?
Don: Of course. We're going to have a barbecue. We're going to cook burgers and potatoes.

Girl: What are we going to wear?
Don: It's a costume party. Everybody's going to wear pirate clothes.
Girl: That sounds like fun.
Don: But bring your swimsuit too. We're going to swim in the pool afterwards.

- Check the answers with the whole class.

Key

Place: 10 Oak Avenue
Date: May 15th
Time: 6.00 p.m.
Eat: barbecue – burgers and potatoes
Wear: pirate clothes
Bring: your swimsuit

 Play the cassette again. Pupils listen and repeat.

- Ask pupils to design their own party invitations, then talk about them in pairs or groups.

Ending the lesson

- Ask questions about pupils' party invitations: *Where's your party going to be?* etc.

Lesson 4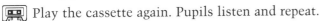

Language	New words and expressions
going to would like to	puppet show, collection, seashell, identify, vegetable patch, plant

Beginning the lesson

- Ask pupils about their plans for the vacation: *Where are they going to go? What would they like to do?* etc.

PB 75 ex 4 **Vacation projects**

What are you planning to do during the summer vacation? Here are some ideas. Talk about them with your friends.

- Look at the pictures and read about what the people are planning to do. Teach the new vocabulary *puppet show, collection, seashell, identify, vegetable patch* and *plant.*

 Play the model dialog on the cassette. Pupils listen and repeat.

- Pupils talk about the pictures in pairs.

- Ask questions with the whole class: *What would you like to do? Would you like to learn to dive? What would you like to learn?*

- Pupils think of their own summer projects and talk about them in pairs or groups.

AB 59 ex D **About this book. Quiz. Write answers to the questions.**

- Ask pupils to do the quiz in pairs or groups. It can be done competitively, to find the group who finish first with the correct answers.

Key

1 Joseph Niepce **2** She/he finds the money to make the movie. **3** Edward Teach **4** in Spain **5** a cannon **6** near the surface of the ocean **7** Yes **8** Because it is dangerous **9** October 1872 **10** in the North Atlantic Ocean **11** A roadie carries the band's equipment. **12** a saxophone **13** a scorpion **14** the bicycle

Ending the lesson

- Ask questions about the summer projects that pupils would like to do: *What would you like to do? Why?*

Project idea

- Museum project: Pupils visit a local museum and draw and write about exhibits which tell them a lot about how people lived in the past.

Assessment activity

- Ask pupils to write answers to the following questions:

  1 What are you going to do during the vacation?
  2 What would you like to put into a time capsule?
  3 Would you like to start a collection?
  4 Who would you like to invite to a party?
  5 What are you going to do this evening?

Language review 6

Lesson 1

> **Language**
> *Simple past*
> *Simple present*
> *future with going to*

Beginning the lesson

- Ask questions about the past, present and future: *When did you learn to ride a bike? Do you ride your bike every day? When are you going to learn to drive?* etc.

 Past, present and future

- Look at the dialogs (*Now you can ...*). Ask pupils to explain what the sentences mean.
- Play the model dialogs on the cassette. Pupils listen and repeat.
- Ask pupils to suggest similar dialogs about their own activities.

 Time expressions. List the time expressions under past and future.

- Ask pupils to write the time expressions in the columns. Check the answers with the class.

  Key

Past	Future
an hour ago	next Wednesday
a hundred years ago	the day after tomorrow
last December	next week
yesterday	next year
in 1860	tomorrow
last week	next month

- Ask pupils to write about themselves, using the correct tense.
- Pupils ask and answer questions in pairs or groups: *Where were you last Saturday?* etc.
- Check pupils' answers with the whole class.

Ending the lesson

- Ask pupils to suggest sentences using the time expressions in exercise A in the Activity Book, e.g. *We came into the room an hour ago.*

Lesson 2

> **Language**   **New words and expressions**
> *Simple past*   badge
> *Simple present*
> *future with going to*

Beginning the lesson

- Ask pupils to explain (in L1) how verbs on the file card on page 77 of the Pupils' Book are formed in the past, present and future.

 Susie has drawn a badge showing her past and her future. What does it mean? Draw a badge for yourself and tell your friend about it.

- Ask pupils to look at the pictures in pairs and suggest sentences about Susie e.g. She learned to play the guitar last year. She bought a guitar last year. She went to Florida last year. Next year she's going to climb a mountain. She's going to get a dog.
- Check the answers with the whole class.
- Pupils draw similar pictures in their own badge, then talk about them in pairs or groups.
- Ask questions about pupils' badges with the whole class.

 Melanie is a famous ice skater. Listen to the interview with her and write *Yes* or *No* answers to the questions.

- Play the cassette, pausing for pupils to write the answers.

  Tapescript

  Man: Hello Melanie.
  Melanie: Hello.
  Man: Melanie, could you tell us some things about yourself? You're a wonderful skater. Do you skate every day?
  Melanie: No, not every day. I don't usually skate on Sundays.
  Man: When did you learn to skate?
  Melanie: Er ... let me see. I had my first lesson four years ago.

Man: Can you tell me something about your life? What are you doing at the moment?

Melanie: I'm very busy at the moment, because I'm entering a competition next month.

Man: Ah yes. Did you win the competition last year?

Melanie: No, I came in second. I want to win the first prize this year.

Man: And what are your plans for next year?

Melanie: Oh, it's very exciting. I'm going to travel to Europe.

Man: You have a very busy life, Melanie. Do you enjoy any other sports besides skating?

Melanie: I'm afraid I don't have time for any other sports. I'd love to learn to ski, but I can't at the moment.

- Check the answers with the whole class.

Key

1 No 2 Yes 3 No 4 No 5 Yes 6 No.

 Play the cassette again. Pupils listen and repeat.

Ending the lesson

- Ask pupils to suggest questions they would like to ask a well known person in an interview.

Lesson 3

Language	New words and expressions
Simple past *Simple present* Future with going to	local, junior

Beginning the lesson

- Ask pupils to think of as many time expressions as they can and list them on the board.

 PB 77 Skills review 6: Reading

Things to do

1 Ask pupils to read the passage and make a list of the sentences in the past, present and future.

- Check the answers with the class.

Key

Past

1 Linda's parents bought her a tennis racket two years ago.
2 She learned to play tennis at the Green Valley Tennis Club.
3 Linda told our reporter about her life as a junior tennis player.

Present

1 I get up at six o'clock to practice.
2 I eat lots of salad and fruit.
3 I drink lots of milk.

Future

1 She is going to play in a big tennis match in Florida next week.
2 Linda's father is going to Florida with her.
3 He's going to watch every game.

- Ask questions about the passage and teach the new words *local* and *junior*.

2 Ask pupils to follow the instructions and play the game in pairs or groups.

3 Pupils make their own file cards with verbs in the past, present and future.

Ending the lesson

- Play the past, present and future game with the whole class.

Lesson 4

Language	New words and expressions
Present perfect Future with going to	disgusting, ranger

Beginning the lesson

- Read the outline for the play on pages 62 and 63 with the class.

AB 62 Let's do a play: The Litter Detectives

- Divide the class into groups. Ask them to discuss and make up dialog to use in each scene in the play. Each group could do a different scene.
- Ask them to practice the scenes in their groups.
- Ask pupils to suggest the props they need to perform the play e.g. items of litter, a bag to collect the litter.
- Practice reading the play, with the extra dialog, with the whole class.
- Practice performing the play.

Ending the lesson

- Pupils perform the play.

Your name _____

A Listen and check (✔) *sometimes* or *usually*.

	sometimes	usually			sometimes	usually
1	☐	☐	6		☐	☐
2	☐	☐	7		☐	☐
3	☐	☐	8		☐	☐
4	☐	☐	9		☐	☐
5	☐	☐	10		☐	☐

10 points

B What would Zoe and Paul like to do on their vacation? Write sentences.

> **Outdoor activities**
>
> Check the things you would like to do.
>
> | **Zoe** | **Paul** |
> |---|---|
> | Photographing birds ✔ | Photographing birds |
> | Playing tennis | Playing tennis ✔ |
> | Learning to dive | Learning to dive ✔ |
> | Building a canoe ✔ | Building a canoe |
> | Looking for ghosts ✔ | Looking for ghosts ✔ |

1 <u>Zoe would like to</u> _____

2 _____

3 _____

4 _____

5 _____

5 points

C Read and match.

1 I couldn't move the table because   **A** it came too early.

2 I couldn't enjoy the movie because   **B** I wasn't old enough.

3 I couldn't catch the bus because   **C** it was too expensive.

4 I couldn't enter the competition because   **D** it wasn't exciting enough.

5 I couldn't buy that camera because   **E** it was too heavy.

5 points

D Write sentences about what they would like to do.

1 *He'd like to climb a mountain.*   2 _____

3 _____   4 _____

_____   _____

5 _____   6 _____

_____   _____

10 points

Your name _____

A Listen and check the dates.

Today is Saturday June 14

	March 14	May 14	June 7	June 12	June 13	June 14
Sue came here.				✔		
Sue bought her hat.						
Jack got his camera.						
Jack's birthday						
Sue's birthday						
Sue met her teacher.						

Write the dates.

1 two days ago   June 12 _____

2 last Saturday   _____

3 a month ago   _____

4 this morning   _____

5 yesterday   _____

6 two months ago   _____

10 points

B Look at the pictures and fill in the gaps with *has, have, hasn't, haven't*.

My friends are waiting for the bus. The bus **hasn't** arrived. The girls _____ bought ice cream cones. They _____ finished eating them. The boy _____ bought an ice cream cone. He _____ bought a sandwich. Some dogs _____ found the sandwich. The boy _____ seen the dogs, but one of the girls _____ seen them.

5 points

C Shopping. Write the conversation.

> I'd like a long sweater, please.

> The longest sweater costs $30.

1 (heavy boots) _____ _____

_____ _____

2 (thick jacket) _____ _____

_____ _____

3 (big hat) _____ _____

_____ _____

4 (short skirt) _____ _____

_____ _____

5 (thick socks) _____ _____

_____ _____

10 points

D Write sentences about the people in the picture.

1 Jack's sister is a beautiful dancer.
She dances beautifully.

2 His brother's a careful driver.

_____

3 His parents are good swimmers.

_____

4 His friend's a bad singer.

_____

5 His grandfather's a careless painter.

_____

6 His grandmother's a quick reader.

_____

10 points

Your name _____

A Listen and write the numbers in the boxes beside the pictures.

A

B

C

D

E

10 points

B How did they go? Write sentences

1 Jane/New York/

Jane went to New York by plane.

2 Henry/school/

_____

3 Gerry's mother/her office/

_____

4 Stan/the desert/

_____

5 Maria/the beach/

_____

6 Dan/the store/

_____ *5 points*

C Ask questions.

1 go into   <u>Can I go into the park, please ?</u>

2 borrow   _____

3 have back   _____

4 play   _____

5 have   _____

6 watch   _____

5 points

D What do they like? Write sentences.

These people are going on vacation. Alex likes camping and he enjoys swimming in the ocean. Jane likes traveling around, but she hates walking and cycling, Peter and Mark like sightseeing. They love cities. Sophie and Joe like taking photos of animals. Ramesh likes walking and climbing mountains. Sharon likes riding her bike.

1 Alex <u>is going to go camping at Sunset Sands.</u>

2 Jane _____

3 Peter and Mark _____

4 Sophie and Joe _____

5 Ramesh _____

6 Sharon _____

10 points

Notes on the tests and key

Teacher's scripts

Exercise A in each test is a listening exercise. Read the script twice: the first time pausing after each sentence and the second time straight through for pupils to check their answers.

Test 1, exercise A

Listen and check *sometimes* or *usually*.

Jack gets up early. He usually has eggs for breakfast and he usually drinks orange juice.
Sometimes, on a Saturday, he has coffee. He usually rides his bicycle to school, but sometimes, when the weather is bad, he takes the bus.
Jack likes photography. Sometimes he buys a photography magazine to read at lunch time. He usually has sandwiches for lunch but sometimes he has salad.
After school Jack usually plays basketball. Sometimes he goes swimming instead.

Test 2, exercise A

Listen and check the dates.

Sue is a new pupil in the class. She's talking to Jack.
Sue came here two days ago, on Thursday.
Sue has a new hat. She bought it this morning.
Jack has a camera. He wants to take a photo of Sue. He got his camera last month, but it wasn't a birthday present.
Jack's birthday was last week. He was twelve last Saturday.
Sue is twelve too. Her birthday was three months ago.
Sue likes her new class. She met the teacher yesterday.

Test 3, exercise A

One. If you wait here, you'll catch the bus.
Two. If you buy two packs of soap, you'll get a T-shirt.
Three. If you go left, you'll find the museum.
Four. If you go right, you'll get to the park.
Five. If you come here next week, you'll see a movie about sharks.

Key

Test 1

A
1 usually 2 usually 3 sometimes 4 usually
5 sometimes 6 sometimes 7 usually 8 sometimes
9 usually 10 sometimes

B
1 Zoe would like to photograph birds.
2 Paul would like to play tennis.
3 Paul would like to learn to dive.
4 Zoe would like to build a canoe.
5 Zoe and Paul would like to look for ghosts.

C
1 E 2 D 3 A 4 B 5 C

D
1 He'd like to climb a mountain.
2 He'd like to eat/have a pizza.
3 It would like to swim in the ocean.
4 They'd like to make a movie.
5 She'd like to ride an elephant.
6 She'd like to go to the beach/read a book.

Test 2

A
Sue came here: June 12; Sue bought her hat: June 14: Jack got his camera; May 14: Jack's birthday: June 7; Sue's birthday: March 14; Sue met the teacher: June 13.
1 June 12 2 June 7 3 May 14 4 June 14
5 June 13 6 April 14

B
My friends are waiting for the bus. The bus *hasn't* arrived. The girls *have* bought ice cream cones. They *haven't* finished eating them. The boy *hasn't* bought an ice cream cone. He *has* bought a sandwich. Some dogs *have* found the sandwich. The boy *hasn't* seen the dogs, but one of the girls *has* seen them.

C
1 I'd like some heavy boots. The heaviest boots cost $39.
2 I'd like a thick jacket. The thickest jacket costs $52.
3 I'd like a big hat. The biggest hat costs $12.
4 I'd like a short skirt. The shortest skirt costs $19.
5 I'd like some thick socks. The thickest socks cost $6.

D
2 He drives carefully.
3 They swim well.
4 He sings badly.
5 He paints carelessly.
6 She reads quickly.

Test 3

A
D1   E2   A3   B4   C5

B

1 Jane went to New York by plane.
2 Henry went to school by bike.
3 Gerry's mother went to her office by car.
4 Stan went to the desert by helicopter.
5 Maria went to the beach by motorcycle.
6 Dan went to the store on foot/Dan walked to the store.

C

1 Can I go into the park, please?
2 Can I borrow your gloves, please?
3 Can I have my kite back, please?
4 Can I play my guitar, please?
5 Can I have a hot dog, please?
6 Can I watch television, please?

D

1 Alex is going to go camping at Sunset Sands.
2 Jane is going to take the train around Europe.
3 Peter and Mark are going to visit London.
4 Sophie and Joe are going to go on safari in Kenya.
5 Ramesh is going to walk in Scotland.
6 Sharon is going to go cycling in Spain.

New words and expressions

Unit 1
bulletin board
photography
photo essay
competition
title
movie studio
entry
enter
star (movie)
early
shed
wildlife
catch (v)
choir
pony
trumpet
clean
Congratulations!
winner
judge
poem
poetry

Unit 2
hole
appear
opposite
modern
press
button
shutter
let in
lens
film
record (v)
nowadays
powerful
object
magnify
X-ray
gun
trick
fire
gallery
trailer
still
thumb
clear
slide
projector
push
pull

Unit 3
fantastic
Be careful!
Action!
Cut!

real
stunt
stunt artist
race car
skydiving
gymnastics
club
movie-making
enormous
Look out!
No entry!
Silence.
in shape
healthy
lemonade
housework
balance
hoop
rescue
scene
lead
wedding
husband
blonde
hate

Language review 1
tuba
file card
file box
encyclopedia
volume

Unit 4
actor/actress
director
camera operator
producer
sound recordist
sound effect
thunderstorm
soldier
march
cellophane
coconut shell
tank
produce
earn

Unit 5
on location
shoot
battle
costume
attack
escape
cannon
fire
special

dream

Unit 6
treasure
sword
coin
flag
chest
gun
belt
coast
fierce
bury
kill
fleet
log book
journey
join
hang
beer
outdoor
creative
mechanical
indoor
studious
type
fix
all-rounder
lifestyle

Language review 2
lost and found
membership

Unit 7
day off
scriptwriter
reef
explore
octopus
grab
disturb
bear
tear
spill
knock over
empty
trash can
mess
goldmine
mining equipment
tool
gold field
block
landslide
sack
turn off
heating
electricity

port
shipwreck

Unit 8
ocean
cover
creature
coral
tiny
mountain range
jellyfish
whale
herring
shark
octopus
ray
jaw
breathe
gently
easily
quickly
lazily
strongly
loudly
carefully
knock
tiptoe
doorstep
suddenly
lid
softly
noisily

Unit 9
discovery
rescue
persuade
mysterious
flipper
narrow
wide
shallow
crowded
comfortable
sailing ship
piece
china
owner
cargo
dish
wooden
as good as new
sink
gold bar
parking lot
meadow
pool
trail

Language review 3
taste
flavor
seaweed
eel

Unit 10
mystery
three-quarters
cover
tiny
solve
puzzle
normal
storm
writer
golden
force
destroy
fact
opinion
maybe
spin
engine
rescue service
lifeboat
life jacket
compass
rescue flare

Unit 11
amazing
desert
weak
river bed
rollerskating
art gallery
dentist
the past week
relax
spend time

Unit 12
rock music
reggae

rap
country music
good at
band
electric guitar
saxophone
flute
go on tour
equipment
sound engineer
lighting engineer
roadie
recording studio
album
video director
storyboard
mime
especially
meter
crazy about
globe
untroubled
free
war

Language review 4
scar
cheek
false teeth
make-up
eyebrows

Unit 13
sunhat
shovel
pick
tape measure
flashlight
metal detector
head for
parachute
airstrip
helicopter pad
vulture
nest

comfortable
cream
pills
playing field
paintbrush
park keeper
ice cream van
picnic area
scorpion
camel
eagle

Unit 14
tennis court
solar power
personal
sidewalk
tortoise
coach
dog sled
continent
Antarctica
steam train
railway locomotive
motor car
diesel engine
burn
poisonous
muscle
magic carpet
broomstick
sail buggy
tractor
insect spray
straight
wire
thread
edge
rod

Unit 15
believe
pace
bend
computer disks

messy
grab
slip
pool
cart
store detective

Unit 16
owl
candlestick
necklace
brooch
earring
time capsule
including
wrapper
meatballs
copy
comic book
air ticket
footprint
adult
barbecue
costume party
puppet show
collection
seashell
identify
vegetable patch
plant

Language review 6
badge
local
junior
disgusting
ranger